King James Version

Psalms & Proverbs

The Book of Psalms

Book I

Psalm 1

[1]Blessed *is* the man that walketh not in the counsel of the ungodly, nor standeth in the way of sinners, nor sitteth in the seat of the scornful.
[2]But his delight *is* in the law of the LORD; and in his law doth he meditate day and night.
[3]And he shall be like a tree planted by the rivers of water, that bringeth forth his fruit in his season; his leaf also shall not wither; and whatsoever he doeth shall prosper.
[4]The ungodly *are* not so: but *are* like the chaff which the wind driveth away.
[5]Therefore the ungodly shall not stand in the judgment, nor sinners in the congregation of the righteous.
[6]For the LORD knoweth the way of the righteous: but the way of the ungodly shall perish.

Psalm 2

[1]Why do the heathen rage, and the people imagine a vain thing?

[2]The kings of the earth set themselves, and the rulers take counsel together, against the LORD, and against his anointed, *saying,*
[3]Let us break their bands asunder, and cast away their cords from us.
[4]He that sitteth in the heavens shall laugh: the Lord shall have them in derision.
[5]Then shall he speak unto them in his wrath, and vex them in his sore displeasure.
[6]Yet have I set my king upon my holy hill of Zion.
[7]I will declare the decree: the LORD hath said unto me, Thou *art* my Son; this day have I begotten thee.
[8]Ask of me, and I shall give *thee* the heathen *for* thine inheritance, and the uttermost parts of the earth *for* thy possession.
[9]Thou shalt break them with a rod of iron; thou shalt dash them in pieces like a potter's vessel.
[10]Be wise now therefore, O ye kings: be instructed, ye judges of the earth.

¹¹Serve the LORD with fear, and rejoice with trembling.
¹²Kiss the Son, lest he be angry, and ye perish *from* the way, when his wrath is kindled but a little. Blessed *are* all they that put their trust in him.

Psalm 3

A Psalm of David, when he fled from Absalom his son.

¹LORD, how are they increased that trouble me! many *are* they that rise up against me.
²Many *there be* which say of my soul, *There is* no help for him in God. Selah.
³But thou, O LORD, *art* a shield for me; my glory, and the lifter up of mine head.
⁴I cried unto the LORD with my voice, and he heard me out of his holy hill. Selah.
⁵I laid me down and slept; I awaked; for the LORD sustained me.
⁶I will not be afraid of ten thousands of people, that have set *themselves* against me round about.
⁷Arise, O LORD; save me, O my God: for thou hast smitten all mine enemies *upon* the cheek bone; thou hast broken the teeth of the ungodly.
⁸Salvation *belongeth* unto the LORD: thy blessing *is* upon thy people. Selah.

Psalm 4

To the chief Musician on Neginoth, A Psalm of David.

¹Hear me when I call, O God of my righteousness: thou hast enlarged me *when I was* in distress; have mercy upon me, and hear my prayer.
²O ye sons of men, how long *will ye turn* my glory into shame? *how long* will ye love vanity, *and* seek after leasing? Selah.
³But know that the LORD hath set apart him that is godly for himself: the LORD will hear when I call unto him.
⁴Stand in awe, and sin not: commune with your own heart upon your bed, and be still. Selah.
⁵Offer the sacrifices of righteousness, and put your trust in the LORD.
⁶*There be* many that say, Who will shew us *any* good? LORD, lift thou up the light of thy countenance upon us.

⁷Thou hast put gladness in my heart, more than in the time *that* their corn and their wine increased.

⁸I will both lay me down in peace, and sleep: for thou, LORD, only makest me dwell in safety.

Psalm 5

To the chief Musician upon Nehiloth, A Psalm of David.

¹Give ear to my words, O LORD, consider my meditation.

²Hearken unto the voice of my cry, my King, and my God: for unto thee will I pray.

³My voice shalt thou hear in the morning, O LORD; in the morning will I direct *my prayer* unto thee, and will look up.

⁴For thou *art* not a God that hath pleasure in wickedness: neither shall evil dwell with thee.

⁵The foolish shall not stand in thy sight: thou hatest all workers of iniquity.

⁶Thou shalt destroy them that speak leasing: the LORD will abhor the bloody and deceitful man.

⁷But as for me, I will come *into* thy house in the multitude of thy mercy: *and* in thy fear will I worship toward thy holy temple.

⁸Lead me, O LORD, in thy righteousness because of mine enemies; make thy way straight before my face.

⁹For *there is* no faithfulness in their mouth; their inward part *is* very wickedness; their throat *is* an open sepulchre; they flatter with their tongue.

¹⁰Destroy thou them, O God; let them fall by their own counsels; cast them out in the multitude of their transgressions; for they have rebelled against thee.

¹¹But let all those that put their trust in thee rejoice: let them ever shout for joy, because thou defendest them: let them also that love thy name be joyful in thee.

¹²For thou, LORD, wilt bless the righteous; with favour wilt thou compass him as *with* a shield.

Psalm 6

To the chief Musician on Neginoth upon Sheminith, A Psalm of David.

¹O LORD, rebuke me not in thine anger, neither chasten me in thy hot displeasure.

²Have mercy upon me, O LORD; for I *am* weak: O LORD, heal me; for my bones are vexed.

³My soul is also sore vexed: but thou, O LORD, how long?

⁴Return, O LORD, deliver my soul: oh save me for thy mercies' sake.

⁵For in death *there is* no remembrance of thee: in the grave who shall give thee thanks?

⁶I am weary with my groaning; all the night make I my bed to swim; I water my couch with my tears.

⁷Mine eye is consumed because of grief; it waxeth old because of all mine enemies.

⁸Depart from me, all ye workers of iniquity; for the LORD hath heard the voice of my weeping.

⁹The LORD hath heard my supplication; the LORD will receive my prayer.

¹⁰Let all mine enemies be ashamed and sore vexed: let them return *and* be ashamed suddenly.

Psalm 7

Shiggaion of David, which he sang unto the LORD, concerning the words of Cush the Benjamite.

¹O Lord my God, in thee do I put my trust: save me from all them that persecute me, and deliver me:

²Lest he tear my soul like a lion, rending *it* in pieces, while *there is* none to deliver.

³O LORD my God, if I have done this; if there be iniquity in my hands;

⁴If I have rewarded evil unto him that was at peace with me; (yea, I have delivered him that without cause is mine enemy:)

⁵Let the enemy persecute my soul, and take *it;* yea, let him tread down my life upon the earth, and lay mine honour in the dust. Selah.

⁶Arise, O LORD, in thine anger, lift up thyself because of the rage of mine enemies: and awake for me *to* the judgment *that* thou hast commanded.

⁷So shall the congregation of the people compass thee about: for their sakes therefore return thou on high.

⁸The LORD shall judge the people: judge me, O LORD, according to my righteousness, and according to mine integrity *that is* in me.

⁹Oh let the wickedness of the wicked come to an end; but establish the just: for the righteous God trieth the hearts and reins.

¹⁰My defence *is* of God, which saveth the upright in heart.

¹¹God judgeth the righteous, and God is angry *with the wicked* every day.

¹²If he turn not, he will whet his sword; he hath bent his bow, and made it ready.

[13]He hath also prepared for him the instruments of death; he ordaineth his arrows against the persecutors.

[14]Behold, he travaileth with iniquity, and hath conceived mischief, and brought forth falsehood.

[15]He made a pit, and digged it, and is fallen into the ditch *which* he made.

[16]His mischief shall return upon his own head, and his violent dealing shall come down upon his own pate.

[17]I will praise the LORD according to his righteousness: and will sing praise to the name of the LORD most high.

Psalm 8

To the chief Musician upon Gittith, A Psalm of David.

[1]O LORD our Lord, how excellent *is* thy name in all the earth! who hast set thy glory above the heavens.

[2]Out of the mouth of babes and sucklings hast thou ordained strength because of thine enemies, that thou mightest still the enemy and the avenger.

[3]When I consider thy heavens, the work of thy fingers, the moon and the stars, which thou hast ordained;

[4]What is man, that thou art mindful of him? and the son of man, that thou visitest him?

[5]For thou hast made him a little lower than the angels, and hast crowned him with glory and honour.

[6]Thou madest him to have dominion over the works of thy hands; thou hast put all *things* under his feet:

[7]All sheep and oxen, yea, and the beasts of the field;

[8]The fowl of the air, and the fish of the sea, *and whatsoever* passeth through the paths of the seas.

[9]O LORD our Lord, how excellent is thy name in all the earth!

Psalm 9

To the chief Musician upon Muthlabben, A Psalm of David.

¹I will praise *thee,* O LORD, with my whole heart; I will shew forth all thy marvellous works.

²I will be glad and rejoice in thee: I will sing praise to thy name, O thou most High.

³When mine enemies are turned back, they shall fall and perish at thy presence.

⁴For thou hast maintained my right and my cause; thou satest in the throne judging right.

⁵Thou hast rebuked the heathen, thou hast destroyed the wicked, thou hast put out their name for ever and ever.

⁶O thou enemy, destructions are come to a perpetual end: and thou hast destroyed cities; their memorial is perished with them.

⁷But the LORD shall endure for ever: he hath prepared his throne for judgment.

⁸And he shall judge the world in righteousness, he shall minister judgment to the people in uprightness.

⁹The LORD also will be a refuge for the oppressed, a refuge in times of trouble.

¹⁰And they that know thy name will put their trust in thee: for thou, LORD, hast not forsaken them that seek thee.

¹¹Sing praises to the LORD, which dwelleth in Zion: declare among the people his doings.

¹²When he maketh inquisition for blood, he remembereth them: he forgetteth not the cry of the humble.

¹³Have mercy upon me, O LORD; consider my trouble *which I suffer* of them that hate me, thou that liftest me up from the gates of death:

¹⁴That I may shew forth all thy praise in the gates of the daughter of Zion: I will rejoice in thy salvation.

¹⁵The heathen are sunk down in the pit *that* they made: in the net which they hid is their own foot taken.

¹⁶The LORD is known *by* the judgment *which* he executeth: the wicked is snared in the work of his own hands. Higgaion. Selah.

¹⁷The wicked shall be turned into hell, *and* all the nations that forget God.

¹⁸For the needy shall not alway be forgotten: the expectation of the poor shall *not* perish for ever.

¹⁹Arise, O LORD; let not man prevail: let the heathen be judged in thy sight.

²⁰Put them in fear, O LORD: *that* the nations may know themselves *to be but* men. Selah.

Psalm 10

¹Why standest thou afar off, O LORD? *why* hidest thou *thyself* in times of trouble?

²The wicked in *his* pride doth persecute the poor: let them be taken in the devices that they have imagined.

³For the wicked boasteth of his heart's desire, and blesseth the covetous, *whom* the LORD abhorreth.

⁴The wicked, through the pride of his countenance, will not seek *after God:* God *is* not in all his thoughts.

⁵His ways are always grievous; thy judgments *are* far above out of his sight: *as for* all his enemies, he puffeth at them.

⁶He hath said in his heart, I shall not be moved: for *I shall* never *be* in adversity.

⁷His mouth is full of cursing and deceit and fraud: under his tongue *is* mischief and vanity.

⁸He sitteth in the lurking places of the villages: in the secret places doth he murder the innocent: his eyes are privily set against the poor.

⁹He lieth in wait secretly as a lion in his den: he lieth in wait to catch the poor: he doth catch the poor, when he draweth him into his net.

¹⁰He croucheth, *and* humbleth himself, that the poor may fall by his strong ones.

¹¹He hath said in his heart, God hath forgotten: he hideth his face; he will never see *it.*

¹²Arise, O LORD; O God, lift up thine hand: forget not the humble.

¹³Wherefore doth the wicked contemn God? he hath said in his heart, Thou wilt not require *it.*

¹⁴Thou hast seen *it;* for thou beholdest mischief and spite, to requite *it* with thy hand: the poor committeth himself unto thee; thou art the helper of the fatherless.

¹⁵Break thou the arm of the wicked and the evil *man:* seek out his wickedness *till* thou find none.

¹⁶The LORD *is* King for ever and ever: the heathen are perished out of his land.

¹⁷LORD, thou hast heard the desire of the humble: thou wilt prepare their heart, thou wilt cause thine ear to hear:

¹⁸To judge the fatherless and the oppressed, that the man of the earth may no more oppress.

Psalm 11

To the chief Musician, A *Psalm* of David.

¹In the LORD put I my trust: How say ye to my soul, Flee *as* a bird to your mountain?

²For, lo, the wicked bend *their* bow, they make ready their arrow upon the string, that they may privily shoot at the upright in heart.

³If the foundations be destroyed, what can the righteous do?

⁴The LORD *is* in his holy temple, the LORD'S throne *is* in heaven: his eyes behold, his eyelids try, the children of men.

⁵The LORD trieth the righteous: but the wicked and him that loveth violence his soul hateth.

⁶Upon the wicked he shall rain snares, fire and brimstone, and an horrible tempest: *this shall be* the portion of their cup.

⁷For the righteous LORD loveth righteousness; his countenance doth behold the upright.

Psalm 12

To the chief Musician upon Sheminith, A Psalm of David.

[1]Help, LORD; for the godly man ceaseth; for the faithful fail from among the children of men.
[2]They speak vanity every one with his neighbour: *with* flattering lips *and* with a double heart do they speak.
[3]The LORD shall cut off all flattering lips, *and* the tongue that speaketh proud things:
[4]Who have said, With our tongue will we prevail; our lips *are* our own: who *is* lord over us?
[5]For the oppression of the poor, for the sighing of the needy, now will I arise, saith the LORD; I will set *him* in safety *from him that* puffeth at him.
[6]The words of the LORD *are* pure words: *as* silver tried in a furnace of earth, purified seven times.
[7]Thou shalt keep them, O LORD, thou shalt preserve them from this generation for ever.
[8]The wicked walk on every side, when the vilest men are exalted.

Psalm 13

To the chief Musician, A Psalm of David.

[1]How long wilt thou forget me, O LORD? for ever? how long wilt thou hide thy face from me?
[2]How long shall I take counsel in my soul, *having* sorrow in my heart daily? how long shall mine enemy be exalted over me?
[3]Consider *and* hear me, O LORD my God: lighten mine eyes, lest I sleep the *sleep of* death;
[4]Lest mine enemy say, I have prevailed against him; *and* those that trouble me rejoice when I am moved.
[5]But I have trusted in thy mercy; my heart shall rejoice in thy salvation.
[6]I will sing unto the LORD, because he hath dealt bountifully with me.

Psalm 14

To the chief Musician, A *Psalm* of David.

[1]The fool hath said in his heart, *There is* no God. They are corrupt, they have done abominable works, *there is* none that doeth good.

[2]The LORD looked down from heaven upon the children of men, to see if there were any that did understand, *and* seek God.

[3]They are all gone aside, they are *all* together become filthy: *there is* none that doeth good, no, not one.

[4]Have all the workers of iniquity no knowledge? who eat up my people *as* they eat bread, and call not upon the LORD.

[5]There were they in great fear: for God *is* in the generation of the righteous.

[6]Ye have shamed the counsel of the poor, because the LORD *is* his refuge.

[7]Oh that the salvation of Israel *were come* out of Zion! when the LORD bringeth back the captivity of his people, Jacob shall rejoice, *and* Israel shall be glad.

Psalm 15

A Psalm of David.

[1]LORD, who shall abide in thy tabernacle? who shall dwell in thy holy hill?

[2]He that walketh uprightly, and worketh righteousness, and speaketh the truth in his heart.

[3]*He that* backbiteth not with his tongue, nor doeth evil to his neighbour, nor taketh up a reproach against his neighbour.

[4]In whose eyes a vile person is contemned; but he honoureth them that fear the LORD. *He that* sweareth to *his own* hurt, and changeth not.

[5]*He that* putteth not out his money to usury, nor taketh reward against the innocent. He that doeth these *things* shall never be moved.

Psalm 16

Michtam of David.

[1]Preserve me, O God: for in thee do I put my trust.
[2]*O my soul,* thou hast said unto the LORD, Thou *art* my Lord: my goodness *extendeth* not to
thee;
[3]*But* to the saints that *are* in the earth, and *to* the excellent, in whom *is* all my delight.
[4]Their sorrows shall be multiplied *that* hasten *after* another *god:* their drink offerings of
blood will I not offer, nor take up their names into my lips.
[5]The LORD *is* the portion of mine inheritance and of my cup: thou maintainest my lot.
[6]The lines are fallen unto me in pleasant *places;* yea, I have a goodly heritage.
[7]I will bless the LORD, who hath given me counsel: my reins also instruct me in the night
seasons.
[8]I have set the LORD always before me: because *he is* at my right hand, I shall not be moved.
[9]Therefore my heart is glad, and my glory rejoiceth: my flesh also shall rest in hope.
[10]For thou wilt not leave my soul in hell; neither wilt thou suffer thine Holy One to see
corruption.
[11]Thou wilt shew me the path of life: in thy presence *is* fulness of joy; at thy right hand *there
are* pleasures for evermore.

Psalm 17

A Prayer of David.

[1]Hear the right, O LORD, attend unto my cry, give ear unto my prayer, *that goeth* not
out of feigned lips.
[2]Let my sentence come forth from thy presence; let thine eyes behold the things that are
equal.
[3]Thou hast proved mine heart; thou hast visited *me* in the night; thou hast tried me, *and* shalt
find nothing; I am purposed *that* my mouth shall not transgress.
[4]Concerning the works of men, by the word of thy lips I have kept *me from* the paths of the
destroyer.
[5]Hold up my goings in thy paths, *that* my footsteps slip not.

⁶I have called upon thee, for thou wilt hear me, O God: incline thine ear unto me, *and hear* my speech.

⁷Shew thy marvellous lovingkindness, O thou that savest by thy right hand them which put their trust *in thee* from those that rise up *against them.*

⁸Keep me as the apple of the eye, hide me under the shadow of thy wings,

⁹From the wicked that oppress me, *from* my deadly enemies, *who* compass me about.

¹⁰They are inclosed in their own fat: with their mouth they speak proudly.

¹¹They have now compassed us in our steps: they have set their eyes bowing down to the earth;

¹²Like as a lion *that* is greedy of his prey, and as it were a young lion lurking in secret places.

¹³Arise, O LORD, disappoint him, cast him down: deliver my soul from the wicked, *which is* thy sword:

¹⁴From men *which are* thy hand, O LORD, from men of the world, *which have* their portion in *this* life, and whose belly thou fillest with thy hid *treasure:* they are full of children, and leave the rest of their *substance* to their babes.

¹⁵As for me, I will behold thy face in righteousness: I shall be satisfied, when I awake, with thy likeness.

Psalm 18

To the chief Musician, A *Psalm* of David, the servant of the LORD, who spake unto the LORD the words of this song in the day *that* the LORD delivered him from the hand of all his enemies, and from the hand of Saul: And he said,

¹I will love thee, O LORD, my strength.

²The LORD *is* my rock, and my fortress, and my deliverer; my God, my strength, in whom I will trust; my buckler, and the horn of my salvation, *and* my high tower.

³I will call upon the LORD, *who is worthy* to be praised: so shall I be saved from mine enemies.

⁴The sorrows of death compassed me, and the floods of ungodly men made me afraid.

⁵The sorrows of hell compassed me about: the snares of death prevented me.

⁶In my distress I called upon the LORD, and cried unto my God: he heard my voice out of his temple, and my cry came before him, *even* into his ears.

⁷Then the earth shook and trembled; the foundations also of the hills moved and were shaken, because he was wroth.

⁸There went up a smoke out of his nostrils, and fire out of his mouth devoured: coals were kindled by it.

⁹He bowed the heavens also, and came down: and darkness *was* under his feet.

¹⁰And he rode upon a cherub, and did fly: yea, he did fly upon the wings of the wind.

¹¹He made darkness his secret place; his pavilion round about him *were* dark waters *and* thick clouds of the skies.

¹²At the brightness *that was* before him his thick clouds passed, hail *stones* and coals of fire.

¹³The LORD also thundered in the heavens, and the Highest gave his voice; hail *stones* and coals of fire.

¹⁴Yea, he sent out his arrows, and scattered them; and he shot out lightnings, and discomfited them.

¹⁵Then the channels of waters were seen, and the foundations of the world were discovered at thy rebuke, O LORD, at the blast of the breath of thy nostrils.

¹⁶He sent from above, he took me, he drew me out of many waters.

¹⁷He delivered me from my strong enemy, and from them which hated me: for they were too strong for me.

¹⁸They prevented me in the day of my calamity: but the LORD was my stay.

¹⁹He brought me forth also into a large place; he delivered me, because he delighted in me.

²⁰The LORD rewarded me according to my righteousness; according to the cleanness of my hands hath he recompensed me.

²¹For I have kept the ways of the LORD, and have not wickedly departed from my God.

²²For all his judgments *were* before me, and I did not put away his statutes from me.

²³I was also upright before him, and I kept myself from mine iniquity.

²⁴Therefore hath the LORD recompensed me according to my righteousness, according to the cleanness of my hands in his eyesight.

²⁵With the merciful thou wilt shew thyself merciful; with an upright man thou wilt shew thyself upright;

²⁶With the pure thou wilt shew thyself pure; and with the froward thou wilt shew thyself froward.

²⁷For thou wilt save the afflicted people; but wilt bring down high looks.

²⁸For thou wilt light my candle: the LORD my God will enlighten my darkness.

²⁹For by thee I have run through a troop; and by my God have I leaped over a wall.

³⁰*As for* God, his way *is* perfect: the word of the LORD is tried: he *is* a buckler to all those that trust in him.

³¹For who *is* God save the LORD? or who *is* a rock save our God?

³²*It is* God that girdeth me with strength, and maketh my way perfect.

³³He maketh my feet like hinds' *feet,* and setteth me upon my high places.

³⁴He teacheth my hands to war, so that a bow of steel is broken by mine arms.

³⁵Thou hast also given me the shield of thy salvation: and thy right hand hath holden me up, and thy gentleness hath made me great.

³⁶Thou hast enlarged my steps under me, that my feet did not slip.

³⁷I have pursued mine enemies, and overtaken them: neither did I turn again till they were consumed.

³⁸I have wounded them that they were not able to rise: they are fallen under my feet.

³⁹For thou hast girded me with strength unto the battle: thou hast subdued under me those that rose up against me.

⁴⁰Thou hast also given me the necks of mine enemies; that I might destroy them that hate me.

⁴¹They cried, but *there was* none to save *them: even* unto the LORD, but he answered them not.

⁴²Then did I beat them small as the dust before the wind: I did cast them out as the dirt in the streets.

⁴³Thou hast delivered me from the strivings of the people; *and* thou hast made me the head of the heathen: a people *whom* I have not known shall serve me.

⁴⁴As soon as they hear of me, they shall obey me: the strangers shall submit themselves unto me.

⁴⁵The strangers shall fade away, and be afraid out of their close places.

⁴⁶The LORD liveth; and blessed *be* my rock; and let the God of my salvation be exalted.

⁴⁷*It is* God that avengeth me, and subdueth the people under me.

⁴⁸He delivereth me from mine enemies: yea, thou liftest me up above those that rise up against me: thou hast delivered me from the violent man.

⁴⁹Therefore will I give thanks unto thee, O LORD, among the heathen, and sing praises unto thy name.

⁵⁰Great deliverance giveth he to his king; and sheweth mercy to his anointed, to David, and to his seed for evermore.

Psalm 19

To the chief Musician, A Psalm of David.

¹The heavens declare the glory of God; and the firmament sheweth his handywork.

²Day unto day uttereth speech, and night unto night sheweth knowledge.

³*There is* no speech nor language, *where* their voice is not heard.

⁴Their line is gone out through all the earth, and their words to the end of the world. In them hath he set a tabernacle for the sun,

⁵Which *is* as a bridegroom coming out of his chamber, *and* rejoiceth as a strong man to run a race.

⁶His going forth *is* from the end of the heaven, and his circuit unto the ends of it: and there is nothing hid from the heat thereof.

⁷The law of the LORD *is* perfect, converting the soul: the testimony of the LORD *is* sure, making wise the simple.

⁸The statutes of the LORD *are* right, rejoicing the heart: the commandment of the LORD *is* pure, enlightening the eyes.

⁹The fear of the LORD *is* clean, enduring for ever: the judgments of the LORD *are* true *and* righteous altogether.

¹⁰More to be desired *are they* than gold, yea, than much fine gold: sweeter also than honey and the honeycomb.

¹¹Moreover by them is thy servant warned: *and* in keeping of them *there is* great reward.

¹²Who can understand *his* errors? cleanse thou me from secret *faults.*

¹³Keep back thy servant also from presumptuous *sins;* let them not have dominion over me: then shall I be upright, and I shall be innocent from the great transgression.

¹⁴Let the words of my mouth, and the meditation of my heart, be acceptable in thy sight, O LORD, my strength, and my redeemer.

Psalm 20

To the chief Musician, A Psalm of David.

¹The LORD hear thee in the day of trouble; the name of the God of Jacob defend thee;

²Send thee help from the sanctuary, and strengthen thee out of Zion;

³Remember all thy offerings, and accept thy burnt sacrifice; Selah.

⁴Grant thee according to thine own heart, and fulfil all thy counsel.

⁵We will rejoice in thy salvation, and in the name of our God we will set up *our* banners: the LORD fulfil all thy petitions.

⁶Now know I that the LORD saveth his anointed; he will hear him from his holy heaven with the saving strength of his right hand.

⁷Some *trust* in chariots, and some in horses: but we will remember the name of the LORD our God.

⁸They are brought down and fallen: but we are risen, and stand upright.

⁹Save, LORD: let the king hear us when we call.

Psalm 21

To the chief Musician, A Psalm of David.

¹The king shall joy in thy strength, O LORD; and in thy salvation how greatly shall he rejoice!

²Thou hast given him his heart's desire, and hast not withholden the request of his lips. Selah.

³For thou preventest him with the blessings of goodness: thou settest a crown of pure gold on his head.

⁴He asked life of thee, *and* thou gavest *it* him, *even* length of days for ever and ever.

⁵His glory *is* great in thy salvation: honour and majesty hast thou laid upon him.

⁶For thou hast made him most blessed for ever: thou hast made him exceeding glad with thy countenance.

⁷For the king trusteth in the LORD, and through the mercy of the most High he shall not be moved.

⁸Thine hand shall find out all thine enemies: thy right hand shall find out those that hate thee.

⁹Thou shalt make them as a fiery oven in the time of thine anger: the LORD shall swallow them up in his wrath, and the fire shall devour them.

¹⁰Their fruit shalt thou destroy from the earth, and their seed from among the children of men.

¹¹For they intended evil against thee: they imagined a mischievous device, *which* they are not able *to perform.*

¹²Therefore shalt thou make them turn their back, *when* thou shalt make ready *thine arrows* upon thy strings against the face of them.

¹³Be thou exalted, LORD, in thine own strength: *so* will we sing and praise thy power.

Psalm 22

To the chief Musician upon Aijeleth Shahar, A Psalm of David.

¹My God, my God, why hast thou forsaken me? *why art thou so* far from helping me, *and from* the words of my roaring?

²O my God, I cry in the daytime, but thou hearest not; and in the night season, and am not silent.

³But thou *art* holy, *O thou* that inhabitest the praises of Israel.

⁴Our fathers trusted in thee: they trusted, and thou didst deliver them.

⁵They cried unto thee, and were delivered: they trusted in thee, and were not confounded.

⁶But I *am* a worm, and no man; a reproach of men, and despised of the people.

⁷All they that see me laugh me to scorn: they shoot out the lip, they shake the head *saying,*

⁸He trusted on the LORD *that* he would deliver him: let him deliver him, seeing he delighted in him.

⁹But thou *art* he that took me out of the womb: thou didst make me hope *when I was* upon my mother's breasts.

¹⁰I was cast upon thee from the womb: thou *art* my God from my mother's belly.

¹¹Be not far from me; for trouble *is* near; for *there is* none to help.

¹²Many bulls have compassed me: strong *bulls* of Bashan have beset me round.

¹³They gaped upon me *with* their mouths, *as* a ravening and a roaring lion.

¹⁴I am poured out like water, and all my bones are out of joint: my heart is like wax; it is melted in the midst of my bowels.

¹⁵My strength is dried up like a potsherd; and my tongue cleaveth to my jaws; and thou hast brought me into the dust of death.

¹⁶For dogs have compassed me: the assembly of the wicked have inclosed me: they pierced my hands and my feet.

¹⁷I may tell all my bones: they look *and* stare upon me.

¹⁸They part my garments among them, and cast lots upon my vesture.

¹⁹But be not thou far from me, O LORD: O my strength, haste thee to help me.

²⁰Deliver my soul from the sword; my darling from the power of the dog.

²¹Save me from the lion's mouth: for thou hast heard me from the horns of the unicorns.

²²I will declare thy name unto my brethren: in the midst of the congregation will I praise thee.

²³Ye that fear the LORD, praise him; all ye the seed of Jacob, glorify him; and fear him, all ye the seed of Israel.

²⁴For he hath not despised nor abhorred the affliction of the afflicted; neither hath he hid his face from him; but when he cried unto him, he heard.

²⁵My praise *shall be* of thee in the great congregation: I will pay my vows before them that fear him.

²⁶The meek shall eat and be satisfied: they shall praise the LORD that seek him: your heart shall live for ever.

²⁷All the ends of the world shall remember and turn unto the LORD: and all the kindreds of the nations shall worship before thee.

²⁸For the kingdom *is* the LORD'S: and he *is* the governor among the nations.

²⁹All *they that be* fat upon earth shall eat and worship: all they that go down to the dust shall bow before him: and none can keep alive his own soul.

³⁰A seed shall serve him; it shall be accounted to the Lord for a generation.

³¹They shall come, and shall declare his righteousness unto a people that shall be born, that he hath done *this*.

Psalm 23

A Psalm of David.

¹The LORD *is* my shepherd; I shall not want.
²He maketh me to lie down in green pastures: he leadeth me beside the still waters.
³He restoreth my soul: he leadeth me in the paths of righteousness for his name's sake.
⁴Yea, though I walk through the valley of the shadow of death, I will fear no evil: for thou *art* with me; thy rod and thy staff they comfort me.
⁵Thou preparest a table before me in the presence of mine enemies: thou anointest my head with oil; my cup runneth over.
⁶Surely goodness and mercy shall follow me all the days of my life: and I will dwell in the house of the LORD for ever.

Psalm 24

A Psalm of David.

¹The earth *is* the LORD'S, and the fulness thereof; the world, and they that dwell therein.
²For he hath founded it upon the seas, and established it upon the floods.
³Who shall ascend into the hill of the LORD? or who shall stand in his holy place?
⁴He that hath clean hands, and a pure heart; who hath not lifted up his soul unto vanity, nor sworn deceitfully.
⁵He shall receive the blessing from the LORD, and righteousness from the God of his salvation.
⁶This *is* the generation of them that seek him, that seek thy face, O Jacob. Selah.
⁷Lift up your heads, O ye gates; and be ye lift up, ye everlasting doors; and the King of glory shall come in.
⁸Who *is* this King of glory? The LORD strong and mighty, the LORD mighty in battle.
⁹Lift up your heads, O ye gates; even lift *them* up, ye everlasting doors; and the King of glory shall come in.
¹⁰Who is this King of glory? The LORD of hosts, he *is* the King of glory. Selah.

Psalm 25

A *Psalm* of David.

¹Unto thee, O LORD, do I lift up my soul.

²O my God, I trust in thee: let me not be ashamed, let not mine enemies triumph over me.

³Yea, let none that wait on thee be ashamed: let them be ashamed which transgress without cause.

⁴Shew me thy ways, O LORD; teach me thy paths.

⁵Lead me in thy truth, and teach me: for thou *art* the God of my salvation; on thee do I wait all the day.

⁶Remember, O LORD, thy tender mercies and thy lovingkindnesses; for they *have been* ever of old.

⁷Remember not the sins of my youth, nor my transgressions: according to thy mercy remember thou me for thy goodness' sake, O LORD.

⁸Good and upright *is* the LORD: therefore will he teach sinners in the way.

⁹The meek will he guide in judgment: and the meek will he teach his way.

¹⁰All the paths of the LORD *are* mercy and truth unto such as keep his covenant and his testimonies.

¹¹For thy name's sake, O LORD, pardon mine iniquity; for it *is* great.

¹²What man *is* he that feareth the LORD? him shall he teach in the way *that* he shall choose.

¹³His soul shall dwell at ease; and his seed shall inherit the earth.

¹⁴The secret of the LORD *is* with them that fear him; and he will shew them his covenant.

¹⁵Mine eyes *are* ever toward the LORD; for he shall pluck my feet out of the net.

¹⁶Turn thee unto me, and have mercy upon me; for I *am* desolate and afflicted.

¹⁷The troubles of my heart are enlarged: *O* bring thou me out of my distresses.

¹⁸Look upon mine affliction and my pain; and forgive all my sins.

¹⁹Consider mine enemies; for they are many; and they hate me with cruel hatred.

²⁰O keep my soul, and deliver me: let me not be ashamed; for I put my trust in thee.

²¹Let integrity and uprightness preserve me; for I wait on thee.

²²Redeem Israel, O God, out of all his troubles.

Psalm 26

A *Psalm* of David.

¹Judge me, O LORD; for I have walked in mine integrity: I have trusted also in the LORD; *therefore* I shall not slide.

²Examine me, O LORD, and prove me; try my reins and my heart.

³For thy lovingkindness *is* before mine eyes: and I have walked in thy truth.

⁴I have not sat with vain persons, neither will I go in with dissemblers.

⁵I have hated the congregation of evildoers; and will not sit with the wicked.

⁶I will wash mine hands in innocency: so will I compass thine altar, O LORD:

⁷That I may publish with the voice of thanksgiving, and tell of all thy wondrous works.

⁸LORD, I have loved the habitation of thy house, and the place where thine honour dwelleth.

⁹Gather not my soul with sinners, nor my life with bloody men:

¹⁰In whose hands *is* mischief, and their right hand is full of bribes.

¹¹But as for me, I will walk in mine integrity: redeem me, and be merciful unto me.

¹²My foot standeth in an even place: in the congregations will I bless the LORD.

Psalm 27

A *Psalm* of David.

¹The LORD *is* my light and my salvation; whom shall I fear? the LORD *is* the strength of my life; of whom shall I be afraid?

²When the wicked, *even* mine enemies and my foes, came upon me to eat up my flesh, they stumbled and fell.

³Though an host should encamp against me, my heart shall not fear: though war should rise against me, in this *will* I *be* confident.

⁴One *thing* have I desired of the LORD, that will I seek after; that I may dwell in the house of the LORD all the days of my life, to behold the beauty of the LORD, and to enquire in his temple.

⁵For in the time of trouble he shall hide me in his pavilion: in the secret of his tabernacle shall he hide me; he shall set me up upon a rock.

⁶And now shall mine head be lifted up above mine enemies round about me: therefore will I offer in his tabernacle sacrifices of joy; I will sing, yea, I will sing praises unto the LORD.

⁷Hear, O LORD, *when* I cry with my voice: have mercy also upon me, and answer me.

⁸*When thou saidst,* Seek ye my face; my heart said unto thee, Thy face, LORD, will I seek.

⁹Hide not thy face *far* from me; put not thy servant away in anger: thou hast been my help; leave me not, neither forsake me, O God of my salvation.

¹⁰When my father and my mother forsake me, then the LORD will take me up.

¹¹Teach me thy way, O LORD, and lead me in a plain path, because of mine enemies.

¹²Deliver me not over unto the will of mine enemies: for false witnesses are risen up against me, and such as breathe out cruelty.

¹³*I had fainted,* unless I had believed to see the goodness of the LORD in the land of the living.

¹⁴Wait on the LORD: be of good courage, and he shall strengthen thine heart: wait, I say, on the LORD.

Psalm 28

A *Psalm* of David.

¹Unto thee will I cry, O LORD my rock; be not silent to me: lest, *if* thou be silent to me, I become like them that go down into the pit.

²Hear the voice of my supplications, when I cry unto thee, when I lift up my hands toward thy holy oracle.

³Draw me not away with the wicked, and with the workers of iniquity, which speak peace to their neighbours, but mischief *is* in their hearts.

⁴Give them according to their deeds, and according to the wickedness of their endeavours: give them after the work of their hands; render to them their desert.

⁵Because they regard not the works of the LORD, nor the operation of his hands, he shall destroy them, and not build them up.

⁶Blessed *be* the LORD, because he hath heard the voice of my supplications.

⁷The LORD *is* my strength and my shield; my heart trusted in him, and I am helped: therefore my heart greatly rejoiceth; and with my song will I praise him.

⁸The LORD *is* their strength, and he *is* the saving strength of his anointed.

⁹Save thy people, and bless thine inheritance: feed them also, and lift them up for ever.

Psalm 29

A Psalm of David.

¹Give unto the LORD, O ye mighty, give unto the LORD glory and strength.

²Give unto the LORD the glory due unto his name; worship the LORD in the beauty of holiness.

³The voice of the LORD *is* upon the waters: the God of glory thundereth: the LORD *is* upon many waters.

⁴The voice of the LORD *is* powerful; the voice of the LORD *is* full of majesty.

⁵The voice of the LORD breaketh the cedars; yea, the LORD breaketh the cedars of Lebanon.

⁶He maketh them also to skip like a calf; Lebanon and Sirion like a young unicorn.

⁷The voice of the LORD divideth the flames of fire.

⁸The voice of the LORD shaketh the wilderness; the LORD shaketh the wilderness of Kadesh.

⁹The voice of the LORD maketh the hinds to calve, and discovereth the forests: and in his temple doth every one speak of *his* glory.

¹⁰The LORD sitteth upon the flood; yea, the LORD sitteth King for ever.

¹¹The LORD will give strength unto his people; the LORD will bless his people with peace.

Psalm 30

A Psalm *and* Song *at* the dedication of the house of David.

¹I will extol thee, O LORD; for thou hast lifted me up, and hast not made my foes to rejoice over me.

²O LORD my God, I cried unto thee, and thou hast healed me.

³O LORD, thou hast brought up my soul from the grave: thou hast kept me alive, that I should not go down to the pit.

⁴Sing unto the LORD, O ye saints of his, and give thanks at the remembrance of his holiness.

⁵For his anger *endureth but* a moment; in his favour is life: weeping may endure for a night, but joy *cometh* in the morning.

⁶And in my prosperity I said, I shall never be moved.

⁷LORD, by thy favour thou hast made my mountain to stand strong: thou didst hide thy face, *and* I was troubled.

⁸I cried to thee, O LORD; and unto the LORD I made supplication.

⁹What profit *is there* in my blood, when I go down to the pit? Shall the dust praise thee? shall it declare thy truth?

¹⁰Hear, O LORD, and have mercy upon me: LORD, be thou my helper.

¹¹Thou hast turned for me my mourning into dancing: thou hast put off my sackcloth, and girded me with gladness;

¹²To the end that *my* glory may sing praise to thee, and not be silent. O LORD my God, I will give thanks unto thee for ever.

Psalm 31

To the chief Musician, A Psalm of David.

[1]In thee, O LORD, do I put my trust; let me never be ashamed: deliver me in thy righteousness.

[2]Bow down thine ear to me; deliver me speedily: be thou my strong rock, for an house of defence to save me.

[3]For thou *art* my rock and my fortress; therefore for thy name's sake lead me, and guide me.

[4]Pull me out of the net that they have laid privily for me: for thou *art* my strength.

[5]Into thine hand I commit my spirit: thou hast redeemed me, O LORD God of truth.

[6]I have hated them that regard lying vanities: but I trust in the LORD.

[7]I will be glad and rejoice in thy mercy: for thou hast considered my trouble; thou hast known my soul in adversities;

[8]And hast not shut me up into the hand of the enemy: thou hast set my feet in a large room.

[9]Have mercy upon me, O LORD, for I am in trouble: mine eye is consumed with grief, *yea,* my soul and my belly.

[10]For my life is spent with grief, and my years with sighing: my strength faileth because of mine iniquity, and my bones are consumed.

[11]I was a reproach among all mine enemies, but especially among my neighbours, and a fear to mine acquaintance: they that did see me without fled from me.

[12]I am forgotten as a dead man out of mind: I am like a broken vessel.

[13]For I have heard the slander of many: fear *was* on every side: while they took counsel together against me, they devised to take away my life.

[14]But I trusted in thee, O LORD: I said, Thou *art* my God.

[15]My times *are* in thy hand: deliver me from the hand of mine enemies, and from them that persecute me.

[16]Make thy face to shine upon thy servant: save me for thy mercies' sake.

[17]Let me not be ashamed, O LORD; for I have called upon thee: let the wicked be ashamed, *and* let them be silent in the grave.

[18]Let the lying lips be put to silence; which speak grievous things proudly and contemptuously against the righteous.

[19]*Oh* how great *is* thy goodness, which thou hast laid up for them that fear thee; *which* thou hast wrought for them that trust in thee before the sons of men!

[20]Thou shalt hide them in the secret of thy presence from the pride of man: thou shalt keep them secretly in a pavilion from the strife of tongues.

[21]Blessed *be* the LORD: for he hath shewed me his marvellous kindness in a strong city.

²²For I said in my haste, I am cut off from before thine eyes: nevertheless thou heardest the voice of my supplications when I cried unto thee.

²³O love the LORD, all ye his saints: *for* the LORD preserveth the faithful, and plentifully rewardeth the proud doer.

²⁴Be of good courage, and he shall strengthen your heart, all ye that hope in the LORD.

Psalm 32

A *Psalm* of David, Maschil.

¹Blessed *is he whose* transgression *is* forgiven, *whose* sin *is* covered.

²Blessed *is* the man unto whom the LORD imputeth not iniquity, and in whose spirit *there is* no guile.

³When I kept silence, my bones waxed old through my roaring all the day long.

⁴For day and night thy hand was heavy upon me: my moisture is turned into the drought of summer. Selah.

⁵I acknowledged my sin unto thee, and mine iniquity have I not hid. I said, I will confess my transgressions unto the LORD; and thou forgavest the iniquity of my sin. Selah.

⁶For this shall every one that is godly pray unto thee in a time when thou mayest be found: surely in the floods of great waters they shall not come nigh unto him.

⁷Thou *art* my hiding place; thou shalt preserve me from trouble; thou shalt compass me about with songs of deliverance. Selah.

⁸I will instruct thee and teach thee in the way which thou shalt go: I will guide thee with mine eye.

⁹Be ye not as the horse, *or* as the mule, *which* have no understanding: whose mouth must be held in with bit and bridle, lest they come near unto thee.

¹⁰Many sorrows *shall be* to the wicked: but he that trusteth in the LORD, mercy shall compass him about.

¹¹Be glad in the LORD, and rejoice, ye righteous: and shout for joy, all *ye that are* upright in heart.

Psalm 33

¹Rejoice in the LORD, O ye righteous: *for* praise is comely for the upright.

²Praise the LORD with harp: sing unto him with the psaltery *and* an instrument of ten strings.

³Sing unto him a new song; play skilfully with a loud noise.

⁴For the word of the LORD *is* right; and all his works *are done* in truth.

⁵He loveth righteousness and judgment: the earth is full of the goodness of the LORD.

⁶By the word of the LORD were the heavens made; and all the host of them by the breath of his mouth.

⁷He gathereth the waters of the sea together as an heap: he layeth up the depth in storehouses.

⁸Let all the earth fear the LORD: let all the inhabitants of the world stand in awe of him.

⁹For he spake, and it was *done;* he commanded, and it stood fast.

¹⁰The LORD bringeth the counsel of the heathen to nought: he maketh the devices of the people of none effect.

¹¹The counsel of the LORD standeth for ever, the thoughts of his heart to all generations.

¹²Blessed *is* the nation whose God *is* the LORD: *and* the people *whom* he hath chosen for his own inheritance.

¹³The LORD looketh from heaven; he beholdeth all the sons of men.

¹⁴From the place of his habitation he looketh upon all the inhabitants of the earth.

¹⁵He fashioneth their hearts alike; he considereth all their works.

¹⁶There is no king saved by the multitude of an host: a mighty man is not delivered by much strength.

¹⁷An horse *is* a vain thing for safety: neither shall he deliver *any* by his great strength.

¹⁸Behold, the eye of the LORD *is* upon them that fear him, upon them that hope in his mercy;

¹⁹To deliver their soul from death, and to keep them alive in famine.

²⁰Our soul waiteth for the LORD: he *is* our help and our shield.

²¹For our heart shall rejoice in him, because we have trusted in his holy name.

²²Let thy mercy, O LORD, be upon us, according as we hope in thee.

Psalm 34

A *Psalm* of David, when he changed his behaviour before Abimelech; who drove him away, and he departed.

¹I will bless the LORD at all times: his praise *shall* continually *be* in my mouth.

²My soul shall make her boast in the LORD: the humble shall hear *thereof,* and be glad.

³O magnify the LORD with me, and let us exalt his name together.

⁴I sought the LORD, and he heard me, and delivered me from all my fears.

⁵They looked unto him, and were lightened: and their faces were not ashamed.

⁶This poor man cried, and the LORD heard *him,* and saved him out of all his troubles.

⁷The angel of the LORD encampeth round about them that fear him, and delivereth them.

[8]O taste and see that the LORD *is* good: blessed *is* the man *that* trusteth in him.

[9]O fear the LORD, ye his saints: for *there is* no want to them that fear him.

[10]The young lions do lack, and suffer hunger: but they that seek the LORD shall not want any good *thing.*

[11]Come, ye children, hearken unto me: I will teach you the fear of the LORD.

[12]What man *is he that* desireth life, *and* loveth *many* days, that he may see good?

[13]Keep thy tongue from evil, and thy lips from speaking guile.

[14]Depart from evil, and do good; seek peace, and pursue it.

[15]The eyes of the LORD *are* upon the righteous, and his ears *are open* unto their cry.

[16]The face of the LORD *is* against them that do evil, to cut off the remembrance of them from the earth.

[17]*The righteous* cry, and the LORD heareth, and delivereth them out of all their troubles.

[18]The LORD *is* nigh unto them that are of a broken heart; and saveth such as be of a contrite spirit.

[19]Many *are* the afflictions of the righteous: but the LORD delivereth him out of them all.

[20]He keepeth all his bones: not one of them is broken.

[21]Evil shall slay the wicked: and they that hate the righteous shall be desolate.

[22]The LORD redeemeth the soul of his servants: and none of them that trust in him shall be desolate.

Psalm 35

A *Psalm* of David.

[1]Plead *my cause,* O LORD, with them that strive with me: fight against them that fight against me.

[2]Take hold of shield and buckler, and stand up for mine help.

[3]Draw out also the spear, and stop *the way* against them that persecute me: say unto my soul, I *am* thy salvation.

[4]Let them be confounded and put to shame that seek after my soul: let them be turned back and brought to confusion that devise my hurt.

[5]Let them be as chaff before the wind: and let the angel of the LORD chase *them.*

[6]Let their way be dark and slippery: and let the angel of the LORD persecute them.

[7]For without cause have they hid for me their net *in* a pit, *which* without cause they have digged for my soul.

[8]Let destruction come upon him at unawares; and let his net that he hath hid catch himself: into that very destruction let him fall.

⁹And my soul shall be joyful in the LORD: it shall rejoice in his salvation.

¹⁰All my bones shall say, LORD, who *is* like unto thee, which deliverest the poor from him that is too strong for him, yea, the poor and the needy from him that spoileth him?

¹¹False witnesses did rise up; they laid to my charge *things* that I knew not.

¹²They rewarded me evil for good *to* the spoiling of my soul.

¹³But as for me, when they were sick, my clothing *was* sackcloth: I humbled my soul with fasting; and my prayer returned into mine own bosom.

¹⁴I behaved myself as though *he had been* my friend *or* brother: I bowed down heavily, as one that mourneth *for his* mother.

¹⁵But in mine adversity they rejoiced, and gathered themselves together: *yea,* the abjects gathered themselves together against me, and I knew *it* not; they did tear *me,* and ceased not:

¹⁶With hypocritical mockers in feasts, they gnashed upon me with their teeth.

¹⁷Lord, how long wilt thou look on? rescue my soul from their destructions, my darling from the lions.

¹⁸I will give thee thanks in the great congregation: I will praise thee among much people.

¹⁹Let not them that are mine enemies wrongfully rejoice over me: *neither* let them wink with the eye that hate me without a cause.

²⁰For they speak not peace: but they devise deceitful matters against *them that are* quiet in the land.

²¹Yea, they opened their mouth wide against me, *and* said, Aha, aha, our eye hath seen *it.*

²²*This* thou hast seen, O LORD: keep not silence: O Lord, be not far from me.

²³Stir up thyself, and awake to my judgment, *even* unto my cause, my God and my Lord.

²⁴Judge me, O LORD my God, according to thy righteousness; and let them not rejoice over me.

²⁵Let them not say in their hearts, Ah, so would we have it: let them not say, We have swallowed him up.

²⁶Let them be ashamed and brought to confusion together that rejoice at mine hurt: let them be clothed with shame and dishonour that magnify *themselves* against me.

²⁷Let them shout for joy, and be glad, that favour my righteous cause: yea, let them say continually, Let the LORD be magnified, which hath pleasure in the prosperity of his servant.

²⁸And my tongue shall speak of thy righteousness *and* of thy praise all the day long.

Psalm 36

To the chief Musician, A *Psalm* of David, the servant of the LORD.

[1]The transgression of the wicked saith within my heart, *that there is* no fear of God before his eyes.

[2]For he flattereth himself in his own eyes, until his iniquity be found to be hateful.

[3]The words of his mouth *are* iniquity and deceit: he hath left off to be wise, *and* to do good.

[4]He deviseth mischief upon his bed; he setteth himself in a way *that is* not good; he abhorreth not evil.

[5]Thy mercy, O LORD, *is* in the heavens; *and* thy faithfulness *reacheth* unto the clouds.

[6]Thy righteousness *is* like the great mountains; thy judgments *are* a great deep: O LORD, thou preservest man and beast.

[7]How excellent *is* thy lovingkindness, O God! therefore the children of men put their trust under the shadow of thy wings.

[8]They shall be abundantly satisfied with the fatness of thy house; and thou shalt make them drink of the river of thy pleasures.

[9]For with thee *is* the fountain of life: in thy light shall we see light.

[10]O continue thy lovingkindness unto them that know thee; and thy righteousness to the upright in heart.

[11]Let not the foot of pride come against me, and let not the hand of the wicked remove me.

[12]There are the workers of iniquity fallen: they are cast down, and shall not be able to rise.

Psalm 37

A *Psalm* of David.

[1]Fret not thyself because of evildoers, neither be thou envious against the workers of iniquity.

[2]For they shall soon be cut down like the grass, and wither as the green herb.

[3]Trust in the LORD, and do good; *so* shalt thou dwell in the land, and verily thou shalt be fed.

[4]Delight thyself also in the LORD; and he shall give thee the desires of thine heart.

[5]Commit thy way unto the LORD; trust also in him; and he shall bring *it* to pass.

[6]And he shall bring forth thy righteousness as the light, and thy judgment as the noonday.

[7]Rest in the LORD, and wait patiently for him: fret not thyself because of him who prospereth in his way, because of the man who bringeth wicked devices to pass.

[8]Cease from anger, and forsake wrath: fret not thyself in any wise to do evil.

[9]For evildoers shall be cut off: but those that wait upon the LORD, they shall inherit the earth.

¹⁰For yet a little while, and the wicked *shall* not *be:* yea, thou shalt diligently consider his place, and it *shall* not *be.*

¹¹But the meek shall inherit the earth; and shall delight themselves in the abundance of peace.

¹²The wicked plotteth against the just, and gnasheth upon him with his teeth.

¹³The Lord shall laugh at him: for he seeth that his day is coming.

¹⁴The wicked have drawn out the sword, and have bent their bow, to cast down the poor and needy, *and* to slay such as be of upright conversation.

¹⁵Their sword shall enter into their own heart, and their bows shall be broken.

¹⁶A little that a righteous man hath *is* better than the riches of many wicked.

¹⁷For the arms of the wicked shall be broken: but the LORD upholdeth the righteous.

¹⁸The LORD knoweth the days of the upright: and their inheritance shall be for ever.

¹⁹They shall not be ashamed in the evil time: and in the days of famine they shall be satisfied.

²⁰But the wicked shall perish, and the enemies of the LORD *shall be* as the fat of lambs: they shall consume; into smoke shall they consume away.

²¹The wicked borroweth, and payeth not again: but the righteous sheweth mercy, and giveth.

²²For *such as be* blessed of him shall inherit the earth; and *they that be* cursed of him shall be cut off.

²³The steps of a *good* man are ordered by the LORD: and he delighteth in his way.

²⁴Though he fall, he shall not be utterly cast down: for the LORD upholdeth *him with* his hand.

²⁵I have been young, and *now* am old; yet have I not seen the righteous forsaken, nor his seed begging bread.

²⁶*He is* ever merciful, and lendeth; and his seed *is* blessed.

²⁷Depart from evil, and do good; and dwell for evermore.

²⁸For the LORD loveth judgment, and forsaketh not his saints; they are preserved for ever: but the seed of the wicked shall be cut off.

²⁹The righteous shall inherit the land, and dwell therein for ever.

³⁰The mouth of the righteous speaketh wisdom, and his tongue talketh of judgment.

³¹The law of his God *is* in his heart; none of his steps shall slide.

³²The wicked watcheth the righteous, and seeketh to slay him.

³³The LORD will not leave him in his hand, nor condemn him when he is judged.

³⁴Wait on the LORD, and keep his way, and he shall exalt thee to inherit the land: when the wicked are cut off, thou shalt see *it.*

³⁵I have seen the wicked in great power, and spreading himself like a green bay tree.

³⁶Yet he passed away, and, lo, he *was* not: yea, I sought him, but he could not be found.

³⁷Mark the perfect *man,* and behold the upright: for the end of *that* man *is* peace.

³⁸But the transgressors shall be destroyed together: the end of the wicked shall be cut off.

³⁹But the salvation of the righteous *is* of the LORD: *he is* their strength in the time of trouble.

⁴⁰And the LORD shall help them and deliver them: he shall deliver them from the wicked, and save them, because they trust in him.

Psalm 38

A Psalm of David, to bring to remembrance.

[1]O LORD, rebuke me not in thy wrath: neither chasten me in thy hot displeasure.

[2]For thine arrows stick fast in me, and thy hand presseth me sore.

[3]*There is* no soundness in my flesh because of thine anger; neither *is there any* rest in my bones because of my sin.

[4]For mine iniquities are gone over mine head: as an heavy burden they are too heavy for me.

[5]My wounds stink *and* are corrupt because of my foolishness.

[6]I am troubled; I am bowed down greatly; I go mourning all the day long.

[7]For my loins are filled with a loathsome *disease:* and *there is* no soundness in my flesh.

[8]I am feeble and sore broken: I have roared by reason of the disquietness of my heart.

[9]Lord, all my desire *is* before thee; and my groaning is not hid from thee.

[10]My heart panteth, my strength faileth me: as for the light of mine eyes, it also is gone from me.

[11]My lovers and my friends stand aloof from my sore; and my kinsmen stand afar off.

[12]They also that seek after my life lay snares *for me:* and they that seek my hurt speak mischievous things, and imagine deceits all the day long.

[13]But I, as a deaf *man,* heard not; and *I was* as a dumb man *that* openeth not his mouth.

[14]Thus I was as a man that heareth not, and in whose mouth *are* no reproofs.

[15]For in thee, O LORD, do I hope: thou wilt hear, O Lord my God.

[16]For I said, *Hear me,* lest *otherwise* they should rejoice over me: when my foot slippeth, they magnify *themselves* against me.

[17]For I *am* ready to halt, and my sorrow *is* continually before me.

[18]For I will declare mine iniquity; I will be sorry for my sin.

[19]But mine enemies *are* lively, *and* they are strong: and they that hate me wrongfully are multiplied.

[20]They also that render evil for good are mine adversaries; because I follow *the thing that good is.*

[21]Forsake me not, O LORD: O my God, be not far from me.

[22]Make haste to help me, O Lord my salvation.

Psalm 39

To the chief Musician, *even* to Jeduthun, A Psalm of David.

[1]I said, I will take heed to my ways, that I sin not with my tongue: I will keep my mouth with a bridle, while the wicked is before me.

[2]I was dumb with silence, I held my peace, *even* from good; and my sorrow was stirred.

[3]My heart was hot within me, while I was musing the fire burned: *then* spake I with my tongue,

[4]LORD, make me to know mine end, and the measure of my days, what it *is; that* I may know how frail I *am.*

[5]Behold, thou hast made my days *as* an handbreadth; and mine age *is* as nothing before thee: verily every man at his best state *is* altogether vanity. Selah.

[6]Surely every man walketh in a vain shew: surely they are disquieted in vain: he heapeth up *riches,* and knoweth not who shall gather them.

[7]And now, Lord, what wait I for? my hope *is* in thee.

[8]Deliver me from all my transgressions: make me not the reproach of the foolish.

[9]I was dumb, I opened not my mouth; because thou didst *it.*

[10]Remove thy stroke away from me: I am consumed by the blow of thine hand.

[11]When thou with rebukes dost correct man for iniquity, thou makest his beauty to consume away like a moth: surely every man *is* vanity. Selah.

[12]Hear my prayer, O LORD, and give ear unto my cry; hold not thy peace at my tears: for I *am* a stranger with thee, *and* a sojourner, as all my fathers *were.*

[13]O spare me, that I may recover strength, before I go hence, and be no more.

Psalm 40

To the chief Musician, A Psalm of David.

[1]I waited patiently for the LORD; and he inclined unto me, and heard my cry.

[2]He brought me up also out of an horrible pit, out of the miry clay, and set my feet upon a rock, *and* established my goings.

[3]And he hath put a new song in my mouth, *even* praise unto our God: many shall see *it,* and fear, and shall trust in the LORD.

[4]Blessed *is* that man that maketh the LORD his trust, and respecteth not the proud, nor such as turn aside to lies.

[5]Many, O LORD my God, *are* thy wonderful works *which* thou hast done, and thy thoughts *which are* to us-ward: they cannot be reckoned up in order unto thee: *if* I would declare and speak *of them,* they are more than can be numbered.

[6]Sacrifice and offering thou didst not desire; mine ears hast thou opened: burnt offering and sin offering hast thou not required.

[7]Then said I, Lo, I come: in the volume of the book *it is* written of me,

[8]I delight to do thy will, O my God: yea, thy law *is* within my heart.

[9]I have preached righteousness in the great congregation: lo, I have not refrained my lips, O LORD, thou knowest.

[10]I have not hid thy righteousness within my heart; I have declared thy faithfulness and thy salvation: I have not concealed thy lovingkindness and thy truth from the great congregation.

[11]Withhold not thou thy tender mercies from me, O LORD: let thy lovingkindness and thy truth continually preserve me.

[12]For innumerable evils have compassed me about: mine iniquities have taken hold upon me, so that I am not able to look up; they are more than the hairs of mine head: therefore my heart faileth me.

[13]Be pleased, O LORD, to deliver me: O LORD, make haste to help me.

[14]Let them be ashamed and confounded together that seek after my soul to destroy it; let them be driven backward and put to shame that wish me evil.

[15]Let them be desolate for a reward of their shame that say unto me, Aha, aha.

[16]Let all those that seek thee rejoice and be glad in thee: let such as love thy salvation say continually, The LORD be magnified.

[17]But I *am* poor and needy; *yet* the Lord thinketh upon me: thou *art* my help and my deliverer; make no tarrying, O my God.

Psalm 41

To the chief Musician, A Psalm of David.

[1]Blessed *is* he that considereth the poor: the LORD will deliver him in time of trouble.

[2]The LORD will preserve him, and keep him alive; *and* he shall be blessed upon the earth: and thou wilt not deliver him unto the will of his enemies.

[3]The LORD will strengthen him upon the bed of languishing: thou wilt make all his bed in his sickness.

⁴I said, LORD, be merciful unto me: heal my soul; for I have sinned against thee.

⁵Mine enemies speak evil of me, When shall he die, and his name perish?

⁶And if he come to see *me*, he speaketh vanity: his heart gathereth iniquity to itself; *when* he goeth abroad, he telleth *it*.

⁷All that hate me whisper together against me: against me do they devise my hurt.

⁸An evil disease, *say they*, cleaveth fast unto him: and *now* that he lieth he shall rise up no more.

⁹Yea, mine own familiar friend, in whom I trusted, which did eat of my bread, hath lifted up *his* heel against me.

¹⁰But thou, O LORD, be merciful unto me, and raise me up, that I may requite them.

¹¹By this I know that thou favourest me, because mine enemy doth not triumph over me.

¹²And as for me, thou upholdest me in mine integrity, and settest me before thy face for ever.

¹³Blessed *be* the LORD God of Israel from everlasting, and to everlasting. Amen, and Amen.

Book II

Psalm 42

To the chief Musician, Maschil, for the sons of Korah.

¹As the hart panteth after the water brooks, so panteth my soul after thee, O God.

²My soul thirsteth for God, for the living God: when shall I come and appear before God?

³My tears have been my meat day and night, while they continually say unto me, Where *is* thy God?

⁴When I remember these *things,* I pour out my soul in me: for I had gone with the multitude, I went with them to the house of God, with the voice of joy and praise, with a multitude that kept holyday.

⁵Why art thou cast down, O my soul? and why *art* thou disquieted in me? hope thou in God: for I shall yet praise him *for* the help of his countenance.

⁶O my God, my soul is cast down within me: therefore will I remember thee from the land of Jordan, and of the Hermonites, from the hill Mizar.

⁷Deep calleth unto deep at the noise of thy waterspouts: all thy waves and thy billows are gone over me.

⁸*Yet* the LORD will command his lovingkindness in the daytime, and in the night his song *shall be* with me, *and* my prayer unto the God of my life.

⁹I will say unto God my rock, Why hast thou forgotten me? why go I mourning because of the oppression of the enemy?

¹⁰*As* with a sword in my bones, mine enemies reproach me; while they say daily unto me, Where *is* thy God?

¹¹Why art thou cast down, O my soul? and why art thou disquieted within me? hope thou in God: for I shall yet praise him, *who is* the health of my countenance, and my God.

Psalm 43

¹Judge me, O God, and plead my cause against an ungodly nation: O deliver me from the deceitful and unjust man.

²For thou *art* the God of my strength: why dost thou cast me off? why go I mourning because of the oppression of the enemy?

³O send out thy light and thy truth: let them lead me; let them bring me unto thy holy hill, and to thy tabernacles.

⁴Then will I go unto the altar of God, unto God my exceeding joy: yea, upon the harp will I praise thee, O God my God.

⁵Why art thou cast down, O my soul? and why art thou disquieted within me? hope in God: for I shall yet praise him, *who is* the health of my countenance, and my God.

Psalm 44

To the chief Musician for the sons of Korah, Maschil.

¹We have heard with our ears, O God, our fathers have told us, *what* work thou didst in their days, in the times of old.

²*How* thou didst drive out the heathen with thy hand, and plantedst them; *how* thou didst afflict the people, and cast them out.

³For they got not the land in possession by their own sword, neither did their own arm save them: but thy right hand, and thine arm, and the light of thy countenance, because thou hadst a favour unto them.

⁴Thou art my King, O God: command deliverances for Jacob.

⁵Through thee will we push down our enemies: through thy name will we tread them under that rise up against us.

⁶For I will not trust in my bow, neither shall my sword save me.

⁷But thou hast saved us from our enemies, and hast put them to shame that hated us.

⁸In God we boast all the day long, and praise thy name for ever. Selah.

⁹But thou hast cast off, and put us to shame; and goest not forth with our armies.

¹⁰Thou makest us to turn back from the enemy: and they which hate us spoil for themselves.

¹¹Thou hast given us like sheep *appointed* for meat; and hast scattered us among the heathen.

¹²Thou sellest thy people for nought, and dost not increase *thy wealth* by their price.

¹³Thou makest us a reproach to our neighbours, a scorn and a derision to them that are round about us.

¹⁴Thou makest us a byword among the heathen, a shaking of the head among the people.

¹⁵My confusion *is* continually before me, and the shame of my face hath covered me,

¹⁶For the voice of him that reproacheth and blasphemeth; by reason of the enemy and avenger.

¹⁷All this is come upon us; yet have we not forgotten thee, neither have we dealt falsely in thy covenant.

¹⁸Our heart is not turned back, neither have our steps declined from thy way;

¹⁹Though thou hast sore broken us in the place of dragons, and covered us with the shadow of death.

²⁰If we have forgotten the name of our God, or stretched out our hands to a strange god;

²¹Shall not God search this out? for he knoweth the secrets of the heart.

²²Yea, for thy sake are we killed all the day long; we are counted as sheep for the slaughter.

²³Awake, why sleepest thou, O Lord? arise, cast *us* not off for ever.

²⁴Wherefore hidest thou thy face, *and* forgettest our affliction and our oppression?

²⁵For our soul is bowed down to the dust: our belly cleaveth unto the earth.

²⁶Arise for our help, and redeem us for thy mercies' sake.

Psalm 45

To the chief Musician upon Shoshannim, for the sons of Korah, Maschil, A Song of loves.

¹My heart is inditing a good matter: I speak of the things which I have made touching the king: my tongue *is* the pen of a ready writer.

²Thou art fairer than the children of men: grace is poured into thy lips: therefore God hath blessed thee for ever.

³Gird thy sword upon *thy* thigh, O *most* mighty, with thy glory and thy majesty.

⁴And in thy majesty ride prosperously because of truth and meekness *and* righteousness; and thy right hand shall teach thee terrible things.

⁵Thine arrows *are* sharp in the heart of the king's enemies; *whereby* the people fall under thee.

⁶Thy throne, O God, *is* for ever and ever: the sceptre of thy kingdom *is* a right sceptre.

⁷Thou lovest righteousness, and hatest wickedness: therefore God, thy God, hath anointed thee with the oil of gladness above thy fellows.

⁸All thy garments *smell* of myrrh, and aloes, *and* cassia, out of the ivory palaces, whereby they have made thee glad.

⁹Kings' daughters *were* among thy honourable women: upon thy right hand did stand the queen in gold of Ophir.

¹⁰Hearken, O daughter, and consider, and incline thine ear; forget also thine own people, and thy father's house;

¹¹So shall the king greatly desire thy beauty: for he *is* thy Lord; and worship thou him.

¹²And the daughter of Tyre *shall be there* with a gift; *even* the rich among the people shall intreat thy favour.

¹³The king's daughter *is* all glorious within: her clothing *is* of wrought gold.

¹⁴She shall be brought unto the king in raiment of needlework: the virgins her companions that follow her shall be brought unto thee.

¹⁵With gladness and rejoicing shall they be brought: they shall enter into the king's palace.

¹⁶Instead of thy fathers shall be thy children, whom thou mayest make princes in all the earth.

¹⁷I will make thy name to be remembered in all generations: therefore shall the people praise thee for ever and ever.

Psalm 46

To the chief Musician for the sons of Korah, A Song upon Alamoth.

¹God *is* our refuge and strength, a very present help in trouble.

²Therefore will not we fear, though the earth be removed, and though the mountains be carried into the midst of the sea;

³*Though* the waters thereof roar *and* be troubled, *though* the mountains shake with the swelling thereof. Selah.

⁴*There is* a river, the streams whereof shall make glad the city of God, the holy *place* of the tabernacles of the most High.

⁵God *is* in the midst of her; she shall not be moved: God shall help her, *and that* right early.

⁶The heathen raged, the kingdoms were moved: he uttered his voice, the earth melted.

⁷The LORD of hosts *is* with us; the God of Jacob *is* our refuge. Selah.

⁸Come, behold the works of the LORD, what desolations he hath made in the earth.

⁹He maketh wars to cease unto the end of the earth; he breaketh the bow, and cutteth the spear in sunder; he burneth the chariot in the fire.

¹⁰Be still, and know that I *am* God: I will be exalted among the heathen, I will be exalted in the earth.

¹¹The LORD of hosts *is* with us; the God of Jacob *is* our refuge. Selah.

Psalm 47

To the chief Musician, A Psalm for the sons of Korah.

¹O clap your hands, all ye people; shout unto God with the voice of triumph.

²For the LORD most high *is* terrible; *he is* a great King over all the earth.

³He shall subdue the people under us, and the nations under our feet.

⁴He shall choose our inheritance for us, the excellency of Jacob whom he loved. Selah.

⁵God is gone up with a shout, the LORD with the sound of a trumpet.

⁶Sing praises to God, sing praises: sing praises unto our King, sing praises.

⁷For God *is* the King of all the earth: sing ye praises with understanding.

⁸God reigneth over the heathen: God sitteth upon the throne of his holiness.

⁹The princes of the people are gathered together, *even* the people of the God of Abraham: for the shields of the earth *belong* unto God: he is greatly exalted.

Psalm 48

A Song *and* Psalm for the sons of Korah.

¹Great *is* the LORD, and greatly to be praised in the city of our God, *in* the mountain of his holiness.

²Beautiful for situation, the joy of the whole earth, *is* mount Zion, *on* the sides of the north, the city of the great King.

³God is known in her palaces for a refuge.

⁴For, lo, the kings were assembled, they passed by together.

⁵They saw *it, and* so they marvelled; they were troubled, *and* hasted away.

⁶Fear took hold upon them there, *and* pain, as of a woman in travail.

⁷Thou breakest the ships of Tarshish with an east wind.

⁸As we have heard, so have we seen in the city of the LORD of hosts, in the city of our God: God will establish it for ever. Selah.

⁹We have thought of thy lovingkindness, O God, in the midst of thy temple.

¹⁰According to thy name, O God, so *is* thy praise unto the ends of the earth: thy right hand is full of righteousness.

¹¹Let mount Zion rejoice, let the daughters of Judah be glad, because of thy judgments.

¹²Walk about Zion, and go round about her: tell the towers thereof.

¹³Mark ye well her bulwarks, consider her palaces; that ye may tell *it* to the generation following.

¹⁴For this God *is* our God for ever and ever: he will be our guide *even* unto death.

Psalm 49

To the chief Musician, A Psalm for the sons of Korah.

¹Hear this, all *ye* people; give ear, all *ye* inhabitants of the world:

²Both low and high, rich and poor, together.

³My mouth shall speak of wisdom; and the meditation of my heart *shall be* of understanding.

⁴I will incline mine ear to a parable: I will open my dark saying upon the harp.

⁵Wherefore should I fear in the days of evil, *when* the iniquity of my heels shall compass me about?

⁶They that trust in their wealth, and boast themselves in the multitude of their riches;

⁷None *of them* can by any means redeem his brother, nor give to God a ransom for him:

⁸(For the redemption of their soul *is* precious, and it ceaseth for ever:)

⁹That he should still live for ever, *and* not see corruption.

¹⁰For he seeth *that* wise men die, likewise the fool and the brutish person perish, and leave their wealth to others.

¹¹Their inward thought *is, that* their houses *shall continue* for ever, *and* their dwelling places to all generations; they call *their* lands after their own names.

¹²Nevertheless man *being* in honour abideth not: he is like the beasts *that* perish.

¹³This their way *is* their folly: yet their posterity approve their sayings. Selah.

¹⁴Like sheep they are laid in the grave; death shall feed on them; and the upright shall have dominion over them in the morning; and their beauty shall consume in the grave from their dwelling.

¹⁵But God will redeem my soul from the power of the grave: for he shall receive me. Selah.

¹⁶Be not thou afraid when one is made rich, when the glory of his house is increased;

¹⁷For when he dieth he shall carry nothing away: his glory shall not descend after him.

¹⁸Though while he lived he blessed his soul: and *men* will praise thee, when thou doest well
      to thyself.

¹⁹He shall go to the generation of his fathers; they shall never see light.

²⁰Man *that is* in honour, and understandeth not, is like the beasts *that* perish.

Psalm 50

A Psalm of Asaph.

¹The mighty God, *even* the LORD, hath spoken, and called the earth from the rising of
the sun unto the going down thereof.

²Out of Zion, the perfection of beauty, God hath shined.

³Our God shall come, and shall not keep silence: a fire shall devour before him, and it shall be
      very tempestuous round about him.

⁴He shall call to the heavens from above, and to the earth, that he may judge his people.

⁵Gather my saints together unto me; those that have made a covenant with me by sacrifice.

⁶And the heavens shall declare his righteousness: for God *is* judge himself. Selah.

⁷Hear, O my people, and I will speak; O Israel, and I will testify against thee: I *am* God, *even*
      thy God.

⁸I will not reprove thee for thy sacrifices or thy burnt offerings, *to have been* continually
      before me.

⁹I will take no bullock out of thy house, *nor* he goats out of thy folds.

¹⁰For every beast of the forest *is* mine, *and* the cattle upon a thousand hills.

¹¹I know all the fowls of the mountains: and the wild beasts of the field *are* mine.

¹²If I were hungry, I would not tell thee: for the world *is* mine, and the fulness thereof.

¹³Will I eat the flesh of bulls, or drink the blood of goats?

¹⁴Offer unto God thanksgiving; and pay thy vows unto the most High:

¹⁵And call upon me in the day of trouble: I will deliver thee, and thou shalt glorify me.

¹⁶But unto the wicked God saith, What hast thou to do to declare my statutes, or *that* thou
      shouldest take my covenant in thy mouth?

¹⁷Seeing thou hatest instruction, and castest my words behind thee.

¹⁸When thou sawest a thief, then thou consentedst with him, and hast been partaker with
      adulterers.

¹⁹Thou givest thy mouth to evil, and thy tongue frameth deceit.

²⁰Thou sittest *and* speakest against thy brother; thou slanderest thine own mother's son.

²¹These *things* hast thou done, and I kept silence; thou thoughtest that I was altogether *such
an one* as thyself: *but* I will reprove thee, and set *them* in order before thine eyes.

²²Now consider this, ye that forget God, lest I tear *you* in pieces, and *there be* none to deliver. ²³Whoso offereth praise glorifieth me: and to him that ordereth *his* conversation *aright* will I shew the salvation of God.

Psalm 51

To the chief Musician, A Psalm of David, when Nathan the prophet came unto him, after he had gone in to Bathsheba.

¹Have mercy upon me, O God, according to thy lovingkindness: according unto the multitude of thy tender mercies blot out my transgressions.
²Wash me throughly from mine iniquity, and cleanse me from my sin.
³For I acknowledge my transgressions: and my sin *is* ever before me.
⁴Against thee, thee only, have I sinned, and done *this* evil in thy sight: that thou mightest be justified when thou speakest, *and* be clear when thou judgest.
⁵Behold, I was shapen in iniquity; and in sin did my mother conceive me.
⁶Behold, thou desirest truth in the inward parts: and in the hidden *part* thou shalt make me to know wisdom.
⁷Purge me with hyssop, and I shall be clean: wash me, and I shall be whiter than snow.
⁸Make me to hear joy and gladness; *that* the bones *which* thou hast broken may rejoice.
⁹Hide thy face from my sins, and blot out all mine iniquities.
¹⁰Create in me a clean heart, O God; and renew a right spirit within me.
¹¹Cast me not away from thy presence; and take not thy holy spirit from me.
¹²Restore unto me the joy of thy salvation; and uphold me *with thy* free spirit.
¹³*Then* will I teach transgressors thy ways; and sinners shall be converted unto thee.
¹⁴Deliver me from bloodguiltiness, O God, thou God of my salvation: *and* my tongue shall sing aloud of thy righteousness.
¹⁵O Lord, open thou my lips; and my mouth shall shew forth thy praise.
¹⁶For thou desirest not sacrifice; else would I give *it:* thou delightest not in burnt offering.
¹⁷The sacrifices of God *are* a broken spirit: a broken and a contrite heart, O God, thou wilt not despise.
¹⁸Do good in thy good pleasure unto Zion: build thou the walls of Jerusalem.
¹⁹Then shalt thou be pleased with the sacrifices of righteousness, with burnt offering and whole burnt offering: then shall they offer bullocks upon thine altar.

Psalm 52

To the chief Musician, Maschil, A *Psalm* of David, when Doeg the Edomite came and told Saul, and said unto him, David is come to the house of Ahimelech.

[1]Why boastest thou thyself in mischief, O mighty man? the goodness of God *endureth* continually.

[2]Thy tongue deviseth mischiefs; like a sharp rasor, working deceitfully.

[3]Thou lovest evil more than good; *and* lying rather than to speak righteousness. Selah.

[4]Thou lovest all devouring words, O *thou* deceitful tongue.

[5]God shall likewise destroy thee for ever, he shall take thee away, and pluck thee out of *thy* dwelling place, and root thee out of the land of the living. Selah.

[6]The righteous also shall see, and fear, and shall laugh at him:

[7]Lo, *this is* the man *that* made not God his strength; but trusted in the abundance of his riches, *and* strengthened himself in his wickedness.

[8]But I *am* like a green olive tree in the house of God: I trust in the mercy of God for ever and ever.

[9]I will praise thee for ever, because thou hast done *it:* and I will wait on thy name; for *it is* good before thy saints.

Psalm 53

To the chief Musician upon Mahalath, Maschil, A *Psalm* of David.

[1]The fool hath said in his heart, *There is* no God. Corrupt are they, and have done abominable iniquity: *there is* none that doeth good.

[2]God looked down from heaven upon the children of men, to see if there were *any* that did understand, that did seek God.

[3]Every one of them is gone back: they are altogether become filthy; *there is* none that doeth good, no, not one.

[4]Have the workers of iniquity no knowledge? who eat up my people *as* they eat bread: they have not called upon God.

⁵There were they in great fear, *where* no fear was: for God hath scattered the bones of him that encampeth *against* thee: thou hast put *them* to shame, because God hath despised them.

⁶Oh that the salvation of Israel *were come* out of Zion! When God bringeth back the captivity of his people, Jacob shall rejoice, *and* Israel shall be glad.

Psalm 54

To the chief Musician on Neginoth, Maschil, A *Psalm* of David, when the Ziphims came and said to Saul, Doth not David hide himself with us?

¹Save me, O God, by thy name, and judge me by thy strength.

²Hear my prayer, O God; give ear to the words of my mouth.

³For strangers are risen up against me, and oppressors seek after my soul: they have not set God before them. Selah.

⁴Behold, God *is* mine helper: the Lord *is* with them that uphold my soul.

⁵He shall reward evil unto mine enemies: cut them off in thy truth.

⁶I will freely sacrifice unto thee: I will praise thy name, O LORD; for *it is* good.

⁷For he hath delivered me out of all trouble: and mine eye hath seen *his desire* upon mine enemies.

Psalm 55

To the chief Musician on Neginoth, Maschil, A *Psalm* of David.

¹Give ear to my prayer, O God; and hide not thyself from my supplication.

²Attend unto me, and hear me: I mourn in my complaint, and make a noise;

³Because of the voice of the enemy, because of the oppression of the wicked: for they cast iniquity upon me, and in wrath they hate me.

⁴My heart is sore pained within me: and the terrors of death are fallen upon me.

⁵Fearfulness and trembling are come upon me, and horror hath overwhelmed me.

⁶And I said, Oh that I had wings like a dove! *for then* would I fly away, and be at rest.

⁷Lo, *then* would I wander far off, *and* remain in the wilderness. Selah.

⁸I would hasten my escape from the windy storm *and* tempest.

⁹Destroy, O Lord, *and* divide their tongues: for I have seen violence and strife in the city.

¹⁰Day and night they go about it upon the walls thereof: mischief also and sorrow *are* in the midst of it.

¹¹Wickedness *is* in the midst thereof: deceit and guile depart not from her streets.

¹²For *it was* not an enemy *that* reproached me; then I could have borne *it:* neither *was it* he that hated me *that* did magnify *himself* against me; then I would have hid myself from him:

¹³But *it was* thou, a man mine equal, my guide, and mine acquaintance.

¹⁴We took sweet counsel together, *and* walked unto the house of God in company.

¹⁵Let death seize upon them, *and* let them go down quick into hell: for wickedness is in their dwellings, *and* among them.

¹⁶As for me, I will call upon God; and the LORD shall save me.

¹⁷Evening, and morning, and at noon, will I pray, and cry aloud: and he shall hear my voice.

¹⁸He hath delivered my soul in peace from the battle *that was* against me: for there were many with me.

¹⁹God shall hear, and afflict them, even he that abideth of old. Selah. Because they have no changes, therefore they fear not God.

²⁰He hath put forth his hands against such as be at peace with him: he hath broken his covenant.

²¹*The words* of his mouth were smoother than butter, but war *was* in his heart: his words were softer than oil, yet *were* they drawn swords.

²²Cast thy burden upon the LORD, and he shall sustain thee: he shall never suffer the righteous to be moved.

²³But thou, O God, shalt bring them down into the pit of destruction: bloody and deceitful men shall not live out half their days; but I will trust in thee.

Psalm 56

To the chief Musician upon Jonathelemrechokim, Michtam of David, when the Philistines took him in Gath.

¹Be merciful unto me, O God: for man would swallow me up; he fighting daily oppresseth me.

²Mine enemies would daily swallow *me* up: for *they be* many that fight against me, O thou most High.

³What time I am afraid, I will trust in thee.

⁴In God I will praise his word, in God I have put my trust; I will not fear what flesh can do unto me.

⁵Every day they wrest my words: all their thoughts *are* against me for evil.

⁶They gather themselves together, they hide themselves, they mark my steps, when they wait for my soul.

⁷Shall they escape by iniquity? in *thine* anger cast down the people, O God.

⁸Thou tellest my wanderings: put thou my tears into thy bottle: *are they* not in thy book?

⁹When I cry *unto thee,* then shall mine enemies turn back: this I know; for God *is* for me.

¹⁰In God will I praise *his* word: in the LORD will I praise *his* word.

¹¹In God have I put my trust: I will not be afraid what man can do unto me.

¹²Thy vows *are* upon me, O God: I will render praises unto thee.

¹³For thou hast delivered my soul from death: *wilt* not *thou deliver* my feet from falling, that I may walk before God in the light of the living?

Psalm 57

To the chief Musician, Altaschith, Michtam of David, when he fled from Saul in the cave.

¹Be merciful unto me, O God, be merciful unto me: for my soul trusteth in thee: yea, in the shadow of thy wings will I make my refuge, until *these* calamities be overpast.

²I will cry unto God most high; unto God that performeth *all things* for me.

³He shall send from heaven, and save *from* the reproach of him that would swallow me up. Selah. God shall send forth his mercy and his truth.

⁴My soul *is* among lions: *and* I lie *even among* them that are set on fire, *even* the sons of men, whose teeth *are* spears and arrows, and their tongue a sharp sword.

⁵Be thou exalted, O God, above the heavens; *let* thy glory *be* above all the earth.

⁶They have prepared a net for my steps; my soul is bowed down: they have digged a pit before me, into the midst whereof they are fallen *themselves.* Selah.

⁷My heart is fixed, O God, my heart is fixed: I will sing and give praise.

⁸Awake up, my glory; awake, psaltery and harp: I *myself* will awake early.

⁹I will praise thee, O Lord, among the people: I will sing unto thee among the nations.

¹⁰For thy mercy is great unto the heavens, and thy truth unto the clouds.

¹¹Be thou exalted, O God, above the heavens: *let* thy glory *be* above all the earth.

Psalm 58

To the chief Musician, Altaschith, Michtam of David.

¹Do ye indeed speak righteousness, O congregation? do ye judge uprightly, O ye sons of men?

²Yea, in heart ye work wickedness; ye weigh the violence of your hands in the earth.

³The wicked are estranged from the womb: they go astray as soon as they be born, speaking lies.

⁴Their poison *is* like the poison of a serpent: *they are* like the deaf adder *that* stoppeth her ear;

⁵Which will not hearken to the voice of charmers, charming never so wisely.

⁶Break their teeth, O God, in their mouth: break out the great teeth of the young lions, O LORD.

⁷Let them melt away as waters *which* run continually: *when* he bendeth *his bow to shoot* his arrows, let them be as cut in pieces.

⁸As a snail *which* melteth, let *every one of them* pass away: *like* the untimely birth of a woman, *that* they may not see the sun.

⁹Before your pots can feel the thorns, he shall take them away as with a whirlwind, both living, and in *his* wrath.

¹⁰The righteous shall rejoice when he seeth the vengeance: he shall wash his feet in the blood of the wicked.

¹¹So that a man shall say, Verily *there is* a reward for the righteous: verily he is a God that judgeth in the earth.

Psalm 59

To the chief Musician, Altaschith, Michtam of David; when Saul sent, and they watched the house to kill him.

¹Deliver me from mine enemies, O my God: defend me from them that rise up against me.

²Deliver me from the workers of iniquity, and save me from bloody men.

³For, lo, they lie in wait for my soul: the mighty are gathered against me; not *for* my transgression, nor *for* my sin, O LORD.

[4]They run and prepare themselves without *my* fault: awake to help me, and behold.

[5]Thou therefore, O LORD God of hosts, the God of Israel, awake to visit all the heathen: be not merciful to any wicked transgressors. Selah.

[6]They return at evening: they make a noise like a dog, and go round about the city.

[7]Behold, they belch out with their mouth: swords *are* in their lips: for who, *say they,* doth hear?

[8]But thou, O LORD, shalt laugh at them; thou shalt have all the heathen in derision.

[9]*Because of* his strength will I wait upon thee: for God *is* my defence.

[10]The God of my mercy shall prevent me: God shall let me see *my desire* upon mine enemies.

[11]Slay them not, lest my people forget: scatter them by thy power; and bring them down, O Lord our shield.

[12]*For* the sin of their mouth *and* the words of their lips let them even be taken in their pride: and for cursing and lying *which* they speak.

[13]Consume *them* in wrath, consume *them,* that they *may* not *be:* and let them know that God ruleth in Jacob unto the ends of the earth. Selah.

[14]And at evening let them return; *and* let them make a noise like a dog, and go round about the city.

[15]Let them wander up and down for meat, and grudge if they be not satisfied.

[16]But I will sing of thy power; yea, I will sing aloud of thy mercy in the morning: for thou hast been my defence and refuge in the day of my trouble.

[17]Unto thee, O my strength, will I sing: for God *is* my defence, *and* the God of my mercy.

Psalm 60

To the chief Musician upon Shushan-eduth, Michtam of David, to teach; when he strove with Aram-naharaim and with Aram-zobah, when Joab returned, and smote of Edom in the valley of salt twelve thousand.

[1]O God, thou hast cast us off, thou hast scattered us, thou hast been displeased; O turn thyself to us again.

[2]Thou hast made the earth to tremble; thou hast broken it: heal the breaches thereof; for it shaketh.

[3]Thou hast shewed thy people hard things: thou hast made us to drink the wine of astonishment.

[4]Thou hast given a banner to them that fear thee, that it may be displayed because of the truth. Selah.

[5]That thy beloved may be delivered; save *with* thy right hand, and hear me.

⁶God hath spoken in his holiness; I will rejoice, I will divide Shechem, and mete out the valley of Succoth.

⁷Gilead *is* mine, and Manasseh *is* mine; Ephraim also *is* the strength of mine head; Judah *is* my lawgiver;

⁸Moab *is* my washpot; over Edom will I cast out my shoe: Philistia, triumph thou because of me.

⁹Who will bring me *into* the strong city? who will lead me into Edom?

¹⁰*Wilt* not thou, O God, *which* hadst cast us off? and *thou,* O God, *which* didst not go out with our armies?

¹¹Give us help from trouble: for vain *is* the help of man.

¹²Through God we shall do valiantly: for he *it is that* shall tread down our enemies.

Psalm 61

To the chief Musician upon Neginah, A *Psalm* of David.

¹Hear my cry, O God; attend unto my prayer.

²From the end of the earth will I cry unto thee, when my heart is overwhelmed: lead me to the rock *that* is higher than I.

³For thou hast been a shelter for me, *and* a strong tower from the enemy.

⁴I will abide in thy tabernacle for ever: I will trust in the covert of thy wings. Selah.

⁵For thou, O God, hast heard my vows: thou hast given *me* the heritage of those that fear thy name.

⁶Thou wilt prolong the king's life: *and* his years as many generations.

⁷He shall abide before God for ever: O prepare mercy and truth, *which* may preserve him.

⁸So will I sing praise unto thy name for ever, that I may daily perform my vows.

Psalm 62

To the chief Musician, to Jeduthun, A Psalm of David.

¹Truly my soul waiteth upon God: from him *cometh* my salvation.

²He only *is* my rock and my salvation; *he is* my defence; I shall not be greatly moved.

³How long will ye imagine mischief against a man? ye shall be slain all of you: as a bowing wall *shall ye be, and as* a tottering fence.

⁴They only consult to cast *him* down from his excellency: they delight in lies: they bless with their mouth, but they curse inwardly. Selah.

⁵My soul, wait thou only upon God; for my expectation *is* from him.

⁶He only *is* my rock and my salvation: *he is* my defence; I shall not be moved.

⁷In God *is* my salvation and my glory: the rock of my strength, *and* my refuge, *is* in God.

⁸Trust in him at all times; *ye* people, pour out your heart before him: God *is* a refuge for us. Selah.

⁹Surely men of low degree *are* vanity, *and* men of high degree *are* a lie: to be laid in the balance, they *are* altogether *lighter* than vanity.

¹⁰Trust not in oppression, and become not vain in robbery: if riches increase, set not your heart *upon them.*

¹¹God hath spoken once; twice have I heard this; that power *belongeth* unto God.

¹²Also unto thee, O Lord, *belongeth* mercy: for thou renderest to every man according to his work.

Psalm 63

A Psalm of David, when he was in the wilderness of Judah.

¹O God, thou *art* my God; early will I seek thee: my soul thirsteth for thee, my flesh longeth for thee in a dry and thirsty land, where no water is;

²To see thy power and thy glory, so *as* I have seen thee in the sanctuary.

³Because thy lovingkindness *is* better than life, my lips shall praise thee.

⁴Thus will I bless thee while I live: I will lift up my hands in thy name.

⁵My soul shall be satisfied as *with* marrow and fatness; and my mouth shall praise *thee* with joyful lips:

⁶When I remember thee upon my bed, *and* meditate on thee in the *night* watches.

⁷Because thou hast been my help, therefore in the shadow of thy wings will I rejoice.

⁸My soul followeth hard after thee: thy right hand upholdeth me.

⁹But those *that* seek my soul, to destroy *it,* shall go into the lower parts of the earth.

¹⁰They shall fall by the sword: they shall be a portion for foxes.

¹¹But the king shall rejoice in God; every one that sweareth by him shall glory: but the mouth of them that speak lies shall be stopped.

Psalm 64

To the chief Musician, A Psalm of David.

[1]Hear my voice, O God, in my prayer: preserve my life from fear of the enemy.

[2]Hide me from the secret counsel of the wicked; from the insurrection of the workers of iniquity:

[3]Who whet their tongue like a sword, *and* bend *their bows to shoot* their arrows, *even* bitter words:

[4]That they may shoot in secret at the perfect: suddenly do they shoot at him, and fear not.

[5]They encourage themselves *in* an evil matter: they commune of laying snares privily; they say, Who shall see them?

[6]They search out iniquities; they accomplish a diligent search: both the inward *thought* of every one *of them,* and the heart, *is* deep.

[7]But God shall shoot at them *with* an arrow; suddenly shall they be wounded.

[8]So they shall make their own tongue to fall upon themselves: all that see them shall flee away.

[9]And all men shall fear, and shall declare the work of God; for they shall wisely consider of his doing.

[10]The righteous shall be glad in the LORD, and shall trust in him; and all the upright in heart shall glory.

Psalm 65

To the chief Musician, A Psalm *and* Song of David.

[1]Praise waiteth for thee, O God, in Sion: and unto thee shall the vow be performed.

[2]O thou that hearest prayer, unto thee shall all flesh come.

[3]Iniquities prevail against me: *as for* our transgressions, thou shalt purge them away.

[4]Blessed *is the man whom* thou choosest, and causest to approach *unto thee, that* he may dwell in thy courts: we shall be satisfied with the goodness of thy house, *even* of thy holy temple.

[5]By terrible things in righteousness wilt thou answer us, O God of our salvation; *who art* the confidence of all the ends of the earth, and of them that are afar off *upon* the sea:

⁶Which by his strength setteth fast the mountains; *being* girded with power:

⁷Which stilleth the noise of the seas, the noise of their waves, and the tumult of the people.

⁸They also that dwell in the uttermost parts are afraid at thy tokens: thou makest the outgoings of the morning and evening to rejoice.

⁹Thou visitest the earth, and waterest it: thou greatly enrichest it with the river of God, *which* is full of water: thou preparest them corn, when thou hast so provided for it.

¹⁰Thou waterest the ridges thereof abundantly: thou settlest the furrows thereof: thou makest it soft with showers: thou blessest the springing thereof.

¹¹Thou crownest the year with thy goodness; and thy paths drop fatness.

¹²They drop *upon* the pastures of the wilderness: and the little hills rejoice on every side.

¹³The pastures are clothed with flocks; the valleys also are covered over with corn; they shout for joy, they also sing.

Psalm 66

To the chief Musician, A Song *or* Psalm.

¹Make a joyful noise unto God, all ye lands:

²Sing forth the honour of his name: make his praise glorious.

³Say unto God, How terrible *art thou in* thy works! through the greatness of thy power shall thine enemies submit themselves unto thee.

⁴All the earth shall worship thee, and shall sing unto thee; they shall sing *to* thy name. Selah.

⁵Come and see the works of God: *he is* terrible *in his* doing toward the children of men.

⁶He turned the sea into dry *land:* they went through the flood on foot: there did we rejoice in him.

⁷He ruleth by his power for ever; his eyes behold the nations: let not the rebellious exalt themselves. Selah.

⁸O bless our God, ye people, and make the voice of his praise to be heard:

⁹Which holdeth our soul in life, and suffereth not our feet to be moved.

¹⁰For thou, O God, hast proved us: thou hast tried us, as silver is tried.

¹¹Thou broughtest us into the net; thou laidst affliction upon our loins.

¹²Thou hast caused men to ride over our heads; we went through fire and through water: but thou broughtest us out into a wealthy *place.*

¹³I will go into thy house with burnt offerings: I will pay thee my vows,

¹⁴Which my lips have uttered, and my mouth hath spoken, when I was in trouble.

¹⁵I will offer unto thee burnt sacrifices of fatlings, with the incense of rams; I will offer bullocks with goats. Selah.

¹⁶Come *and* hear, all ye that fear God, and I will declare what he hath done for my soul.
¹⁷I cried unto him with my mouth, and he was extolled with my tongue.
¹⁸If I regard iniquity in my heart, the Lord will not hear *me:*
¹⁹*But* verily God hath heard *me;* he hath attended to the voice of my prayer.
²⁰Blessed *be* God, which hath not turned away my prayer, nor his mercy from me.

Psalm 67

To the chief Musician on Neginoth, A Psalm *or* Song.

¹God be merciful unto us, and bless us; *and* cause his face to shine upon us; Selah.
²That thy way may be known upon earth, thy saving health among all nations.
³Let the people praise thee, O God; let all the people praise thee.
⁴O let the nations be glad and sing for joy: for thou shalt judge the people righteously, and govern the nations upon earth. Selah.
⁵Let the people praise thee, O God; let all the people praise thee.
⁶*Then* shall the earth yield her increase; *and* God, *even* our own God, shall bless us.
⁷God shall bless us; and all the ends of the earth shall fear him.

Psalm 68

To the chief Musician, A Psalm *or* Song of David.

¹Let God arise, let his enemies be scattered: let them also that hate him flee before him.
²As smoke is driven away, *so* drive *them* away: as wax melteth before the fire, *so* let the wicked perish at the presence of God.
³But let the righteous be glad; let them rejoice before God: yea, let them exceedingly rejoice.
⁴Sing unto God, sing praises to his name: extol him that rideth upon the heavens by his name JAH, and rejoice before him.
⁵A father of the fatherless, and a judge of the widows, *is* God in his holy habitation.
⁶God setteth the solitary in families: he bringeth out those which are bound with chains: but the rebellious dwell in a dry *land.*

⁷O God, when thou wentest forth before thy people, when thou didst march through the
wilderness; Selah:

⁸The earth shook, the heavens also dropped at the presence of God: *even* Sinai itself *was
moved* at the presence of God, the God of Israel.

⁹Thou, O God, didst send a plentiful rain, whereby thou didst confirm thine inheritance, when
it was weary.

¹⁰Thy congregation hath dwelt therein: thou, O God, hast prepared of thy goodness for the
poor.

¹¹The Lord gave the word: great *was* the company of those that published *it.*

¹²Kings of armies did flee apace: and she that tarried at home divided the spoil.

¹³Though ye have lien among the pots, *yet shall ye be as* the wings of a dove covered with
silver, and her feathers with yellow gold.

¹⁴When the Almighty scattered kings in it, it was *white* as snow in Salmon.

¹⁵The hill of God *is as* the hill of Bashan; an high hill *as* the hill of Bashan.

¹⁶Why leap ye, ye high hills? *this is* the hill *which* God desireth to dwell in; yea, the LORD
will dwell *in it* for ever.

¹⁷The chariots of God *are* twenty thousand, *even* thousands of angels: the Lord *is* among
them, *as in* Sinai, in the holy *place.*

¹⁸Thou hast ascended on high, thou hast led captivity captive: thou hast received gifts for
men; yea, *for* the rebellious also, that the LORD God might dwell *among them.*

¹⁹Blessed *be* the Lord, *who* daily loadeth us *with benefits, even* the God of our salvation.
Selah.

²⁰*He that is* our God *is* the God of salvation; and unto God the Lord *belong* the issues from
death.

²¹But God shall wound the head of his enemies, *and* the hairy scalp of such an one as goeth
on still in his trespasses.

²²The Lord said, I will bring again from Bashan, I will bring *my people* again from the depths
of the sea:

²³That thy foot may be dipped in the blood of *thine* enemies, *and* the tongue of thy dogs in the
same.

²⁴They have seen thy goings, O God; *even* the goings of my God, my King, in the sanctuary.

²⁵The singers went before, the players on instruments *followed* after; among *them were* the
damsels playing with timbrels.

²⁶Bless ye God in the congregations, *even* the Lord, from the fountain of Israel.

²⁷There *is* little Benjamin *with* their ruler, the princes of Judah *and* their council, the princes
of Zebulun, *and* the princes of Naphtali.

²⁸Thy God hath commanded thy strength: strengthen, O God, that which thou hast wrought
for us.

²⁹Because of thy temple at Jerusalem shall kings bring presents unto thee.

³⁰Rebuke the company of spearmen, the multitude of the bulls, with the calves of the people, *till every one* submit himself with pieces of silver: scatter thou the people *that* delight in war.

³¹Princes shall come out of Egypt; Ethiopia shall soon stretch out her hands unto God.

³²Sing unto God, ye kingdoms of the earth; O sing praises unto the Lord; Selah:

³³To him that rideth upon the heavens of heavens, *which were* of old; lo, he doth send out his voice, *and that* a mighty voice.

³⁴Ascribe ye strength unto God: his excellency *is* over Israel, and his strength *is* in the clouds.

³⁵O God, *thou art* terrible out of thy holy places: the God of Israel *is* he that giveth strength and power unto *his* people. Blessed *be* God.

Psalm 69

To chief Musician upon Shoshannim, A *Psalm* of David.

¹Save me, O God; for the waters are come in unto *my* soul.

²I sink in deep mire, where *there is* no standing: I am come into deep waters, where the floods overflow me.

³I am weary of my crying: my throat is dried: mine eyes fail while I wait for my God.

⁴They that hate me without a cause are more than the hairs of mine head: they that would destroy me, *being* mine enemies wrongfully, are mighty: then I restored *that* which I took not away.

⁵O God, thou knowest my foolishness; and my sins are not hid from thee.

⁶Let not them that wait on thee, O Lord GOD of hosts, be ashamed for my sake: let not those that seek thee be confounded for my sake, O God of Israel.

⁷Because for thy sake I have borne reproach; shame hath covered my face.

⁸I am become a stranger unto my brethren, and an alien unto my mother's children.

⁹For the zeal of thine house hath eaten me up; and the reproaches of them that reproached thee are fallen upon me.

¹⁰When I wept, *and chastened* my soul with fasting, that was to my reproach.

¹¹I made sackcloth also my garment; and I became a proverb to them.

¹²They that sit in the gate speak against me; and I *was* the song of the drunkards.

¹³But as for me, my prayer *is* unto thee, O LORD, *in* an acceptable time: O God, in the multitude of thy mercy hear me, in the truth of thy salvation.

¹⁴Deliver me out of the mire, and let me not sink: let me be delivered from them that hate me, and out of the deep waters.

¹⁵Let not the waterflood overflow me, neither let the deep swallow me up, and let not the pit shut her mouth upon me.

¹⁶Hear me, O LORD; for thy lovingkindness *is* good: turn unto me according to the multitude of thy tender mercies.

¹⁷And hide not thy face from thy servant; for I am in trouble: hear me speedily.

¹⁸Draw nigh unto my soul, *and* redeem it: deliver me because of mine enemies.

¹⁹Thou hast known my reproach, and my shame, and my dishonour: mine adversaries *are* all before thee.

²⁰Reproach hath broken my heart; and I am full of heaviness: and I looked *for some* to take pity, but *there was* none; and for comforters, but I found none.

²¹They gave me also gall for my meat; and in my thirst they gave me vinegar to drink.

²²Let their table become a snare before them: and *that which should have been* for *their* welfare, *let it become* a trap.

²³Let their eyes be darkened, that they see not; and make their loins continually to shake.

²⁴Pour out thine indignation upon them, and let thy wrathful anger take hold of them.

²⁵Let their habitation be desolate; *and* let none dwell in their tents.

²⁶For they persecute *him* whom thou hast smitten; and they talk to the grief of those whom thou hast wounded.

²⁷Add iniquity unto their iniquity: and let them not come into thy righteousness.

²⁸Let them be blotted out of the book of the living, and not be written with the righteous.

²⁹But I *am* poor and sorrowful: let thy salvation, O God, set me up on high.

³⁰I will praise the name of God with a song, and will magnify him with thanksgiving.

³¹*This* also shall please the LORD better than an ox *or* bullock that hath horns and hoofs.

³²The humble shall see *this, and* be glad: and your heart shall live that seek God.

³³For the LORD heareth the poor, and despiseth not his prisoners.

³⁴Let the heaven and earth praise him, the seas, and every thing that moveth therein.

³⁵For God will save Zion, and will build the cities of Judah: that they may dwell there, and have it in possession.

³⁶The seed also of his servants shall inherit it: and they that love his name shall dwell therein.

Psalm 70

To the chief Musician, A *Psalm* of David, to bring to remembrance.

¹*Make haste,* O God, to deliver me; make haste to help me, O LORD.

²Let them be ashamed and confounded that seek after my soul: let them be turned backward, and put to confusion, that desire my hurt.

³Let them be turned back for a reward of their shame that say, Aha, aha.

⁴Let all those that seek thee rejoice and be glad in thee: and let such as love thy salvation say continually, Let God be magnified.

⁵But I *am* poor and needy: make haste unto me, O God: thou *art* my help and my deliverer; O LORD, make no tarrying.

Psalm 71

¹In thee, O LORD, do I put my trust: let me never be put to confusion.

²Deliver me in thy righteousness, and cause me to escape: incline thine ear unto me, and save me.

³Be thou my strong habitation, whereunto I may continually resort: thou hast given commandment to save me; for thou *art* my rock and my fortress.

⁴Deliver me, O my God, out of the hand of the wicked, out of the hand of the unrighteous and cruel man.

⁵For thou *art* my hope, O Lord GOD: *thou art* my trust from my youth.

⁶By thee have I been holden up from the womb: thou art he that took me out of my mother's bowels: my praise *shall be* continually of thee.

⁷I am as a wonder unto many; but thou *art* my strong refuge.

⁸Let my mouth be filled *with* thy praise *and with* thy honour all the day.

⁹Cast me not off in the time of old age; forsake me not when my strength faileth.

¹⁰For mine enemies speak against me; and they that lay wait for my soul take counsel together,

¹¹Saying, God hath forsaken him: persecute and take him; for *there is* none to deliver *him*.

¹²O God, be not far from me: O my God, make haste for my help.

¹³Let them be confounded *and* consumed that are adversaries to my soul; let them be covered *with* reproach and dishonour that seek my hurt.

¹⁴But I will hope continually, and will yet praise thee more and more.

¹⁵My mouth shall shew forth thy righteousness *and* thy salvation all the day; for I know not the numbers *thereof*.

¹⁶I will go in the strength of the Lord GOD: I will make mention of thy righteousness, *even* of thine only.

¹⁷O God, thou hast taught me from my youth: and hitherto have I declared thy wondrous works.

¹⁸Now also when I am old and greyheaded, O God, forsake me not; until I have shewed thy strength unto *this* generation, *and* thy power to every one *that* is to come.

¹⁹Thy righteousness also, O God, *is* very high, who hast done great things: O God, who *is* like unto thee!

20*Thou,* which hast shewed me great and sore troubles, shalt quicken me again, and shalt bring me up again from the depths of the earth.

21Thou shalt increase my greatness, and comfort me on every side.

22I will also praise thee with the psaltery, *even* thy truth, O my God: unto thee will I sing with the harp, O thou Holy One of Israel.

23My lips shall greatly rejoice when I sing unto thee; and my soul, which thou hast redeemed.

24My tongue also shall talk of thy righteousness all the day long: for they are confounded, for they are brought unto shame, that seek my hurt.

Psalm 72

A *Psalm* for Solomon.

1Give the king thy judgments, O God, and thy righteousness unto the king's son.

2He shall judge thy people with righteousness, and thy poor with judgment.

3The mountains shall bring peace to the people, and the little hills, by righteousness.

4He shall judge the poor of the people, he shall save the children of the needy, and shall break in pieces the oppressor.

5They shall fear thee as long as the sun and moon endure, throughout all generations.

6He shall come down like rain upon the mown grass: as showers *that* water the earth.

7In his days shall the righteous flourish; and abundance of peace so long as the moon endureth.

8He shall have dominion also from sea to sea, and from the river unto the ends of the earth.

9They that dwell in the wilderness shall bow before him; and his enemies shall lick the dust.

10The kings of Tarshish and of the isles shall bring presents: the kings of Sheba and Seba shall offer gifts.

11Yea, all kings shall fall down before him: all nations shall serve him.

12For he shall deliver the needy when he crieth; the poor also, and *him* that hath no helper.

13He shall spare the poor and needy, and shall save the souls of the needy.

14He shall redeem their soul from deceit and violence: and precious shall their blood be in his sight.

15And he shall live, and to him shall be given of the gold of Sheba: prayer also shall be made for him continually; *and* daily shall he be praised.

16There shall be an handful of corn in the earth upon the top of the mountains; the fruit thereof shall shake like Lebanon: and *they* of the city shall flourish like grass of the earth.

¹⁷His name shall endure for ever: his name shall be continued as long as the sun: and *men* shall be blessed in him: all nations shall call him blessed.

¹⁸Blessed *be* the LORD God, the God of Israel, who only doeth wondrous things.

¹⁹And blessed *be* his glorious name for ever: and let the whole earth be filled *with* his glory; Amen, and Amen.

²⁰The prayers of David the son of Jesse are ended.

Book III

Psalm 73

A Psalm of Asaph.

¹Truly God *is* good to Israel, *even* to such as are of a clean heart.

²But as for me, my feet were almost gone; my steps had well nigh slipped.

³For I was envious at the foolish, *when* I saw the prosperity of the wicked.

⁴For *there are* no bands in their death: but their strength *is* firm.

⁵They *are* not in trouble *as other* men; neither are they plagued like *other* men.

⁶Therefore pride compasseth them about as a chain; violence covereth them *as* a garment.

⁷Their eyes stand out with fatness: they have more than heart could wish.

⁸They are corrupt, and speak wickedly *concerning* oppression: they speak loftily.

⁹They set their mouth against the heavens, and their tongue walketh through the earth.

¹⁰Therefore his people return hither: and waters of a full *cup* are wrung out to them.

¹¹And they say, How doth God know? and is there knowledge in the most High?

¹²Behold, these *are* the ungodly, who prosper in the world; they increase *in* riches.

¹³Verily I have cleansed my heart *in* vain, and washed my hands in innocency.

¹⁴For all the day long have I been plagued, and chastened every morning.

¹⁵If I say, I will speak thus; behold, I should offend *against* the generation of thy children.

¹⁶When I thought to know this, it *was* too painful for me;

¹⁷Until I went into the sanctuary of God; *then* understood I their end.

¹⁸Surely thou didst set them in slippery places: thou castedst them down into destruction.

¹⁹How are they *brought* into desolation, as in a moment! they are utterly consumed with terrors.

²⁰As a dream when *one* awaketh; *so,* O Lord, when thou awakest, thou shalt despise their image.

²¹Thus my heart was grieved, and I was pricked in my reins.

²²So foolish *was* I, and ignorant: I was *as* a beast before thee.

²³Nevertheless I *am* continually with thee: thou hast holden *me* by my right hand.
²⁴Thou shalt guide me with thy counsel, and afterward receive me *to* glory.
²⁵Whom have I in heaven *but thee?* and *there is* none upon earth *that* I desire beside thee.
²⁶My flesh and my heart faileth: *but* God *is* the strength of my heart, and my portion for ever.
²⁷For, lo, they that are far from thee shall perish: thou hast destroyed all them that go a whoring from thee.
²⁸But *it is* good for me to draw near to God: I have put my trust in the Lord GOD, that I may declare all thy works.

Psalm 74

Maschil of Asaph.

¹O God, why hast thou cast us off for ever? *why* doth thine anger smoke against the sheep of thy pasture?
²Remember thy congregation, *which* thou hast purchased of old; the rod of thine inheritance, *which* thou hast redeemed; this mount Zion, wherein thou hast dwelt.
³Lift up thy feet unto the perpetual desolations; *even* all *that* the enemy hath done wickedly in the sanctuary.
⁴Thine enemies roar in the midst of thy congregations; they set up their ensigns *for* signs.
⁵*A man* was famous according as he had lifted up axes upon the thick trees.
⁶But now they break down the carved work thereof at once with axes and hammers.
⁷They have cast fire into thy sanctuary, they have defiled *by casting down* the dwelling place of thy name to the ground.
⁸They said in their hearts, Let us destroy them together: they have burned up all the synagogues of God in the land.
⁹We see not our signs: *there is* no more any prophet: neither *is there* among us any that knoweth how long.
¹⁰O God, how long shall the adversary reproach? shall the enemy blaspheme thy name for ever?
¹¹Why withdrawest thou thy hand, even thy right hand? pluck *it* out of thy bosom.
¹²For God *is* my King of old, working salvation in the midst of the earth.
¹³Thou didst divide the sea by thy strength: thou brakest the heads of the dragons in the waters.
¹⁴Thou brakest the heads of leviathan in pieces, *and* gavest him *to be* meat to the people inhabiting the wilderness.
¹⁵Thou didst cleave the fountain and the flood: thou driedst up mighty rivers.

¹⁶The day *is* thine, the night also *is* thine: thou hast prepared the light and the sun.

¹⁷Thou hast set all the borders of the earth: thou hast made summer and winter.

¹⁸Remember this, *that* the enemy hath reproached, O LORD, and *that* the foolish people have blasphemed thy name.

¹⁹O deliver not the soul of thy turtledove unto the multitude *of the wicked:* forget not the congregation of thy poor for ever.

²⁰Have respect unto the covenant: for the dark places of the earth are full of the habitations of cruelty.

²¹O let not the oppressed return ashamed: let the poor and needy praise thy name.

²²Arise, O God, plead thine own cause: remember how the foolish man reproacheth thee daily.

²³Forget not the voice of thine enemies: the tumult of those that rise up against thee increaseth continually.

Psalm 75

To the chief Musician, Altaschith, A Psalm *or* Song of Asaph.

¹Unto thee, O God, do we give thanks, *unto thee* do we give thanks: for *that* thy name is near thy wondrous works declare.

²When I shall receive the congregation I will judge uprightly.

³The earth and all the inhabitants thereof are dissolved: I bear up the pillars of it. Selah.

⁴I said unto the fools, Deal not foolishly: and to the wicked, Lift not up the horn:

⁵Lift not up your horn on high: speak *not with* a stiff neck.

⁶For promotion *cometh* neither from the east, nor from the west, nor from the south.

⁷But God *is* the judge: he putteth down one, and setteth up another.

⁸For in the hand of the LORD *there is* a cup, and the wine is red; it is full of mixture; and he poureth out of the same: but the dregs thereof, all the wicked of the earth shall wring *them* out, *and* drink *them.*

⁹But I will declare for ever; I will sing praises to the God of Jacob.

¹⁰All the horns of the wicked also will I cut off; *but* the horns of the righteous shall be exalted.

Psalm 76

To the chief Musician on Neginoth, A Psalm *or* Song of Asaph.

[1]In Judah *is* God known: his name *is* great in Israel.

[2]In Salem also is his tabernacle, and his dwelling place in Zion.

[3]There brake he the arrows of the bow, the shield, and the sword, and the battle. Selah.

[4]Thou *art* more glorious *and* excellent than the mountains of prey.

[5]The stouthearted are spoiled, they have slept their sleep: and none of the men of might have found their hands.

[6]At thy rebuke, O God of Jacob, both the chariot and horse are cast into a dead sleep.

[7]Thou, *even* thou, *art* to be feared: and who may stand in thy sight when once thou art angry?

[8]Thou didst cause judgment to be heard from heaven; the earth feared, and was still,

[9]When God arose to judgment, to save all the meek of the earth. Selah.

[10]Surely the wrath of man shall praise thee: the remainder of wrath shalt thou restrain.

[11]Vow, and pay unto the LORD your God: let all that be round about him bring presents unto him that ought to be feared.

[12]He shall cut off the spirit of princes: *he is* terrible to the kings of the earth.

Psalm 77

To the chief Musician, to Jeduthun, A Psalm of Asaph.

[1]I cried unto God with my voice, *even* unto God with my voice; and he gave ear unto me.

[2]In the day of my trouble I sought the Lord: my sore ran in the night, and ceased not: my soul refused to be comforted.

[3]I remembered God, and was troubled: I complained, and my spirit was overwhelmed. Selah.

[4]Thou holdest mine eyes waking: I am so troubled that I cannot speak.

[5]I have considered the days of old, the years of ancient times.

[6]I call to remembrance my song in the night: I commune with mine own heart: and my spirit made diligent search.

[7]Will the Lord cast off for ever? and will he be favourable no more?

[8]Is his mercy clean gone for ever? doth *his* promise fail for evermore?

[9]Hath God forgotten to be gracious? hath he in anger shut up his tender mercies? Selah.

[10]And I said, This *is* my infirmity: *but I will remember* the years of the right hand of the most High.

[11]I will remember the works of the LORD: surely I will remember thy wonders of old.

[12]I will meditate also of all thy work, and talk of thy doings.

¹³Thy way, O God, *is* in the sanctuary: who *is so* great a God as *our* God?

¹⁴Thou *art* the God that doest wonders: thou hast declared thy strength among the people.

¹⁵Thou hast with *thine* arm redeemed thy people, the sons of Jacob and Joseph. Selah.

¹⁶The waters saw thee, O God, the waters saw thee; they were afraid: the depths also were troubled.

¹⁷The clouds poured out water: the skies sent out a sound: thine arrows also went abroad.

¹⁸The voice of thy thunder *was* in the heaven: the lightnings lightened the world: the earth trembled and shook.

¹⁹Thy way *is* in the sea, and thy path in the great waters, and thy footsteps are not known.

²⁰Thou leddest thy people like a flock by the hand of Moses and Aaron.

Psalm 78

Maschil of Asaph.

¹Give ear, O my people, *to* my law: incline your ears to the words of my mouth.

²I will open my mouth in a parable: I will utter dark sayings of old:

³Which we have heard and known, and our fathers have told us.

⁴We will not hide *them* from their children, shewing to the generation to come the praises of the LORD, and his strength, and his wonderful works that he hath done.

⁵For he established a testimony in Jacob, and appointed a law in Israel, which he commanded our fathers, that they should make them known to their children:

⁶That the generation to come might know *them, even* the children *which* should be born; *who* should arise and declare *them* to their children:

⁷That they might set their hope in God, and not forget the works of God, but keep his commandments:

⁸And might not be as their fathers, a stubborn and rebellious generation; a generation *that* set not their heart aright, and whose spirit was not stedfast with God.

⁹The children of Ephraim, *being* armed, *and* carrying bows, turned back in the day of battle.

¹⁰They kept not the covenant of God, and refused to walk in his law;

¹¹And forgat his works, and his wonders that he had shewed them.

¹²Marvellous things did he in the sight of their fathers, in the land of Egypt, *in* the field of Zoan.

¹³He divided the sea, and caused them to pass through; and he made the waters to stand as an heap.

¹⁴In the daytime also he led them with a cloud, and all the night with a light of fire.

¹⁵He clave the rocks in the wilderness, and gave *them* drink as *out of* the great depths.

¹⁶He brought streams also out of the rock, and caused waters to run down like rivers.

¹⁷And they sinned yet more against him by provoking the most High in the wilderness.

¹⁸And they tempted God in their heart by asking meat for their lust.

¹⁹Yea, they spake against God; they said, Can God furnish a table in the wilderness?

²⁰Behold, he smote the rock, that the waters gushed out, and the streams overflowed; can he give bread also? can he provide flesh for his people?

²¹Therefore the LORD heard *this,* and was wroth: so a fire was kindled against Jacob, and anger also came up against Israel;

²²Because they believed not in God, and trusted not in his salvation:

²³Though he had commanded the clouds from above, and opened the doors of heaven,

²⁴And had rained down manna upon them to eat, and had given them of the corn of heaven.

²⁵Man did eat angels' food: he sent them meat to the full.

²⁶He caused an east wind to blow in the heaven: and by his power he brought in the south wind.

²⁷He rained flesh also upon them as dust, and feathered fowls like as the sand of the sea:

²⁸And he let *it* fall in the midst of their camp, round about their habitations.

²⁹So they did eat, and were well filled: for he gave them their own desire;

³⁰They were not estranged from their lust. But while their meat *was* yet in their mouths,

³¹The wrath of God came upon them, and slew the fattest of them, and smote down the chosen *men* of Israel.

³²For all this they sinned still, and believed not for his wondrous works.

³³Therefore their days did he consume in vanity, and their years in trouble.

³⁴When he slew them, then they sought him: and they returned and enquired early after God.

³⁵And they remembered that God *was* their rock, and the high God their redeemer.

³⁶Nevertheless they did flatter him with their mouth, and they lied unto him with their tongues.

³⁷For their heart was not right with him, neither were they stedfast in his covenant.

³⁸But he, *being* full of compassion, forgave *their* iniquity, and destroyed *them* not: yea, many a time turned he his anger away, and did not stir up all his wrath.

³⁹For he remembered that they *were but* flesh; a wind that passeth away, and cometh not again.

⁴⁰How oft did they provoke him in the wilderness, *and* grieve him in the desert!

⁴¹Yea, they turned back and tempted God, and limited the Holy One of Israel.

⁴²They remembered not his hand, *nor* the day when he delivered them from the enemy.

⁴³How he had wrought his signs in Egypt, and his wonders in the field of Zoan:

⁴⁴And had turned their rivers into blood; and their floods, that they could not drink.

⁴⁵He sent divers sorts of flies among them, which devoured them; and frogs, which destroyed them.

⁴⁶He gave also their increase unto the caterpiller, and their labour unto the locust.

⁴⁷He destroyed their vines with hail, and their sycomore trees with frost.

⁴⁸He gave up their cattle also to the hail, and their flocks to hot thunderbolts.

⁴⁹He cast upon them the fierceness of his anger, wrath, and indignation, and trouble, by sending evil angels *among them.*

⁵⁰He made a way to his anger; he spared not their soul from death, but gave their life over to the pestilence;

⁵¹And smote all the firstborn in Egypt; the chief of *their* strength in the tabernacles of Ham:

⁵²But made his own people to go forth like sheep, and guided them in the wilderness like a flock.

⁵³And he led them on safely, so that they feared not: but the sea overwhelmed their enemies.

⁵⁴And he brought them to the border of his sanctuary, *even to* this mountain, *which* his right hand had purchased.

⁵⁵He cast out the heathen also before them, and divided them an inheritance by line, and made the tribes of Israel to dwell in their tents.

⁵⁶Yet they tempted and provoked the most high God, and kept not his testimonies:

⁵⁷But turned back, and dealt unfaithfully like their fathers: they were turned aside like a deceitful bow.

⁵⁸For they provoked him to anger with their high places, and moved him to jealousy with their graven images.

⁵⁹When God heard *this,* he was wroth, and greatly abhorred Israel:

⁶⁰So that he forsook the tabernacle of Shiloh, the tent *which* he placed among men;

⁶¹And delivered his strength into captivity, and his glory into the enemy's hand.

⁶²He gave his people over also unto the sword; and was wroth with his inheritance.

⁶³The fire consumed their young men; and their maidens were not given to marriage.

⁶⁴Their priests fell by the sword; and their widows made no lamentation.

⁶⁵Then the Lord awaked as one out of sleep, *and* like a mighty man that shouteth by reason of wine.

⁶⁶And he smote his enemies in the hinder parts: he put them to a perpetual reproach.

⁶⁷Moreover he refused the tabernacle of Joseph, and chose not the tribe of Ephraim:

⁶⁸But chose the tribe of Judah, the mount Zion which he loved.

⁶⁹And he built his sanctuary like high *palaces,* like the earth which he hath established for ever.

⁷⁰He chose David also his servant, and took him from the sheepfolds:

⁷¹From following the ewes great with young he brought him to feed Jacob his people, and Israel his inheritance.

⁷²So he fed them according to the integrity of his heart; and guided them by the skilfulness of his hands.

Psalm 79

A Psalm of Asaph.

[1]O God, the heathen are come into thine inheritance; thy holy temple have they defiled; they have laid Jerusalem on heaps.

[2]The dead bodies of thy servants have they given *to be* meat unto the fowls of the heaven, the flesh of thy saints unto the beasts of the earth.

[3]Their blood have they shed like water round about Jerusalem; and *there was* none to bury *them.*

[4]We are become a reproach to our neighbours, a scorn and derision to them that are round about us.

[5]How long, LORD? wilt thou be angry for ever? shall thy jealousy burn like fire?

[6]Pour out thy wrath upon the heathen that have not known thee, and upon the kingdoms that have not called upon thy name.

[7]For they have devoured Jacob, and laid waste his dwelling place.

[8]O remember not against us former iniquities: let thy tender mercies speedily prevent us: for we are brought very low.

[9]Help us, O God of our salvation, for the glory of thy name: and deliver us, and purge away our sins, for thy name's sake.

[10]Wherefore should the heathen say, Where *is* their God? let him be known among the heathen in our sight *by* the revenging of the blood of thy servants *which is* shed.

[11]Let the sighing of the prisoner come before thee; according to the greatness of thy power preserve thou those that are appointed to die;

[12]And render unto our neighbours sevenfold into their bosom their reproach, wherewith they have reproached thee, O Lord.

[13]So we thy people and sheep of thy pasture will give thee thanks for ever: we will shew forth thy praise to all generations.

Psalm 80

To the chief Musician upon Shoshannim-Eduth, A Psalm of Asaph.

¹Give ear, O Shepherd of Israel, thou that leadest Joseph like a flock; thou that dwellest *between* the cherubims, shine forth.

²Before Ephraim and Benjamin and Manasseh stir up thy strength, and come *and* save us.

³Turn us again, O God, and cause thy face to shine; and we shall be saved.

⁴O LORD God of hosts, how long wilt thou be angry against the prayer of thy people?

⁵Thou feedest them with the bread of tears; and givest them tears to drink in great measure.

⁶Thou makest us a strife unto our neighbours: and our enemies laugh among themselves.

⁷Turn us again, O God of hosts, and cause thy face to shine; and we shall be saved.

⁸Thou hast brought a vine out of Egypt: thou hast cast out the heathen, and planted it.

⁹Thou preparedst *room* before it, and didst cause it to take deep root, and it filled the land.

¹⁰The hills were covered with the shadow of it, and the boughs thereof *were like* the goodly cedars.

¹¹She sent out her boughs unto the sea, and her branches unto the river.

¹²Why hast thou *then* broken down her hedges, so that all they which pass by the way do pluck her?

¹³The boar out of the wood doth waste it, and the wild beast of the field doth devour it.

¹⁴Return, we beseech thee, O God of hosts: look down from heaven, and behold, and visit this vine;

¹⁵And the vineyard which thy right hand hath planted, and the branch *that* thou madest strong for thyself.

¹⁶*It is* burned with fire, *it is* cut down: they perish at the rebuke of thy countenance.

¹⁷Let thy hand be upon the man of thy right hand, upon the son of man *whom* thou madest strong for thyself.

¹⁸So will not we go back from thee: quicken us, and we will call upon thy name.

¹⁹Turn us again, O LORD God of hosts, cause thy face to shine; and we shall be saved.

Psalm 81

To the chief Musician upon Gittith, a Psalm of Asaph.

¹Sing aloud unto God our strength: make a joyful noise unto the God of Jacob.

²Take a psalm, and bring hither the timbrel, the pleasant harp with the psaltery.

³Blow up the trumpet in the new moon, in the time appointed, on our solemn feast day.

⁴For this *was* a statute for Israel, *and* a law of the God of Jacob.

⁵This he ordained in Joseph *for* a testimony, when he went out through the land of Egypt: *where* I heard a language *that* I understood not.

⁶I removed his shoulder from the burden: his hands were delivered from the pots.

⁷Thou calledst in trouble, and I delivered thee; I answered thee in the secret place of thunder: I proved thee at the waters of Meribah. Selah.

⁸Hear, O my people, and I will testify unto thee: O Israel, if thou wilt hearken unto me;

⁹There shall no strange god be in thee; neither shalt thou worship any strange god.

¹⁰I *am* the LORD thy God, which brought thee out of the land of Egypt: open thy mouth wide, and I will fill it.

¹¹But my people would not hearken to my voice; and Israel would none of me.

¹²So I gave them up unto their own hearts' lust: *and* they walked in their own counsels.

¹³Oh that my people had hearkened unto me, *and* Israel had walked in my ways!

¹⁴I should soon have subdued their enemies, and turned my hand against their adversaries.

¹⁵The haters of the LORD should have submitted themselves unto him: but their time should have endured for ever.

¹⁶He should have fed them also with the finest of the wheat: and with honey out of the rock should I have satisfied thee.

Psalm 82

A Psalm of Asaph.

¹God standeth in the congregation of the mighty; he judgeth among the gods.

²How long will ye judge unjustly, and accept the persons of the wicked? Selah.

³Defend the poor and fatherless: do justice to the afflicted and needy.

⁴Deliver the poor and needy: rid *them* out of the hand of the wicked.

⁵They know not, neither will they understand; they walk on in darkness: all the foundations of the earth are out of course.

⁶I have said, Ye *are* gods; and all of you *are* children of the most High.

⁷But ye shall die like men, and fall like one of the princes.

⁸Arise, O God, judge the earth: for thou shalt inherit all nations.

Psalm 83

A Song *or* Psalm of Asaph.

¹Keep not thou silence, O God: hold not thy peace, and be not still, O God.

²For, lo, thine enemies make a tumult: and they that hate thee have lifted up the head.

³They have taken crafty counsel against thy people, and consulted against thy hidden ones.

⁴They have said, Come, and let us cut them off from *being* a nation; that the name of Israel may be no more in remembrance.

⁵For they have consulted together with one consent: they are confederate against thee:

⁶The tabernacles of Edom, and the Ishmaelites; of Moab, and the Hagarenes;

⁷Gebal, and Ammon, and Amalek; the Philistines with the inhabitants of Tyre;

⁸Assur also is joined with them: they have holpen the children of Lot. Selah.

⁹Do unto them as *unto* the Midianites; as *to* Sisera, as *to* Jabin, at the brook of Kison:

¹⁰*Which* perished at Endor: they became *as* dung for the earth.

¹¹Make their nobles like Oreb, and like Zeeb: yea, all their princes as Zebah, and as Zalmunna:

¹²Who said, Let us take to ourselves the houses of God in possession.

¹³O my God, make them like a wheel; as the stubble before the wind.

¹⁴As the fire burneth a wood, and as the flame setteth the mountains on fire;

¹⁵So persecute them with thy tempest, and make them afraid with thy storm.

¹⁶Fill their faces with shame; that they may seek thy name, O LORD.

¹⁷Let them be confounded and troubled for ever; yea, let them be put to shame, and perish:

¹⁸That *men* may know that thou, whose name alone *is* JEHOVAH, *art* the most high over all the earth.

Psalm 84

To the chief Musician upon Gittith, A Psalm for the sons of Korah.

¹How amiable *are* thy tabernacles, O LORD of hosts!

²My soul longeth, yea, even fainteth for the courts of the LORD: my heart and my flesh crieth out for the living God.

³Yea, the sparrow hath found an house, and the swallow a nest for herself, where she may lay her young, *even* thine altars, O LORD of hosts, my King, and my God.

⁴Blessed *are* they that dwell in thy house: they will be still praising thee. Selah.

⁵Blessed *is* the man whose strength *is* in thee; in whose heart *are* the ways *of them.*

⁶*Who* passing through the valley of Baca make it a well; the rain also filleth the pools.

⁷They go from strength to strength, *every one of them* in Zion appeareth before God.

⁸O LORD God of hosts, hear my prayer: give ear, O God of Jacob. Selah.

⁹Behold, O God our shield, and look upon the face of thine anointed.

¹⁰For a day in thy courts *is* better than a thousand. I had rather be a doorkeeper in the house of my God, than to dwell in the tents of wickedness.

¹¹For the LORD God *is* a sun and shield: the LORD will give grace and glory: no good *thing* will he withhold from them that walk uprightly.

¹²O LORD of hosts, blessed *is* the man that trusteth in thee.

Psalm 85

To the chief Musician, A Psalm for the sons of Korah.

¹LORD, thou hast been favourable unto thy land: thou hast brought back the captivity of Jacob.

²Thou hast forgiven the iniquity of thy people, thou hast covered all their sin. Selah.

³Thou hast taken away all thy wrath: thou hast turned *thyself* from the fierceness of thine anger.

⁴Turn us, O God of our salvation, and cause thine anger toward us to cease.

⁵Wilt thou be angry with us for ever? wilt thou draw out thine anger to all generations?

⁶Wilt thou not revive us again: that thy people may rejoice in thee?

⁷Shew us thy mercy, O LORD, and grant us thy salvation.

⁸I will hear what God the LORD will speak: for he will speak peace unto his people, and to his saints: but let them not turn again to folly.

⁹Surely his salvation *is* nigh them that fear him; that glory may dwell in our land.

¹⁰Mercy and truth are met together; righteousness and peace have kissed *each other.*

¹¹Truth shall spring out of the earth; and righteousness shall look down from heaven.

¹²Yea, the LORD shall give *that which is* good; and our land shall yield her increase.

¹³Righteousness shall go before him; and shall set *us* in the way of his steps.

Psalm 86

A Prayer of David.

¹Bow down thine ear, O LORD, hear me: for I *am* poor and needy.

²Preserve my soul; for I *am* holy: O thou my God, save thy servant that trusteth in thee.

³Be merciful unto me, O Lord: for I cry unto thee daily.

⁴Rejoice the soul of thy servant: for unto thee, O Lord, do I lift up my soul.

⁵For thou, Lord, *art* good, and ready to forgive; and plenteous in mercy unto all them that call upon thee.

⁶Give ear, O LORD, unto my prayer; and attend to the voice of my supplications.

⁷In the day of my trouble I will call upon thee: for thou wilt answer me.

⁸Among the gods *there is* none like unto thee, O Lord; neither *are there any works* like unto thy works.

⁹All nations whom thou hast made shall come and worship before thee, O Lord; and shall glorify thy name.

¹⁰For thou *art* great, and doest wondrous things: thou *art* God alone.

¹¹Teach me thy way, O LORD; I will walk in thy truth: unite my heart to fear thy name.

¹²I will praise thee, O Lord my God, with all my heart: and I will glorify thy name for evermore.

¹³For great *is* thy mercy toward me: and thou hast delivered my soul from the lowest hell.

¹⁴O God, the proud are risen against me, and the assemblies of violent *men* have sought after my soul; and have not set thee before them.

¹⁵But thou, O Lord, *art* a God full of compassion, and gracious, longsuffering, and plenteous in mercy and truth.

¹⁶O turn unto me, and have mercy upon me; give thy strength unto thy servant, and save the son of thine handmaid.

¹⁷Show me a token for good; that they which hate me may see *it,* and be ashamed: because thou, LORD, hast helped me, and comforted me.

Psalm 87

A Psalm *or* Song for the sons of Korah.

¹His foundation *is* in the holy mountains.

²The LORD loveth the gates of Zion more than all the dwellings of Jacob.

³Glorious things are spoken of thee, O city of God. Selah.

⁴I will make mention of Rahab and Babylon to them that know me: behold Philistia, and Tyre, with Ethiopia; this *man* was born there.

⁵And of Zion it shall be said, This and *that man* was born in her: and the highest himself shall establish her.

⁶The LORD shall count, when he writeth up the people, that this man was born there. Selah.

⁷As well the singers as the players on instruments *shall be there:* all my springs *are* in thee.

Psalm 88

A Song *or* Psalm for the sons of Korah, to the chief Musician upon Mahalath Leannoth, Maschil of Heman the Ezrahite.

[1]O LORD God of my salvation, I have cried day *and* night before thee:
[2]Let my prayer come before thee: incline thine ear unto my cry;
[3]For my soul is full of troubles: and my life draweth nigh unto the grave.
[4]I am counted with them that go down into the pit: I am as a man *that hath* no strength:
[5]Free among the dead, like the slain that lie in the grave, whom thou rememberest no more: and they are cut off from thy hand.
[6]Thou hast laid me in the lowest pit, in darkness, in the deeps.
[7]Thy wrath lieth hard upon me, and thou hast afflicted *me* with all thy waves. Selah.
[8]Thou hast put away mine acquaintance far from me; thou hast made me an abomination unto them: *I am* shut up, and I cannot come forth.
[9]Mine eye mourneth by reason of affliction: LORD, I have called daily upon thee, I have stretched out my hands unto thee.
[10]Wilt thou shew wonders to the dead? shall the dead arise *and* praise thee? Selah.
[11]Shall thy lovingkindness be declared in the grave? *or* thy faithfulness in destruction?
[12]Shall thy wonders be known in the dark? and thy righteousness in the land of forgetfulness?
[13]But unto thee have I cried, O LORD; and in the morning shall my prayer prevent thee.
[14]LORD, why castest thou off my soul? *why* hidest thou thy face from me?
[15]I *am* afflicted and ready to die from *my* youth up: *while* I suffer thy terrors I am distracted.
[16]Thy fierce wrath goeth over me; thy terrors have cut me off.
[17]They came round about me daily like water; they compassed me about together.
[18]Lover and friend hast thou put far from me, *and* mine acquaintance into darkness.

Psalm 89

Maschil of Ethan the Ezrahite.

¹I will sing of the mercies of the LORD for ever: with my mouth will I make known thy faithfulness to all generations.

²For I have said, Mercy shall be built up for ever: thy faithfulness shalt thou establish in the very heavens.

³I have made a covenant with my chosen, I have sworn unto David my servant,

⁴Thy seed will I establish for ever, and build up thy throne to all generations. Selah.

⁵And the heavens shall praise thy wonders, O LORD: thy faithfulness also in the congregation of the saints.

⁶For who in the heaven can be compared unto the LORD? *who* among the sons of the mighty can be likened unto the LORD?

⁷God is greatly to be feared in the assembly of the saints, and to be had in reverence of all *them that are* about him.

⁸O LORD God of hosts, who *is* a strong LORD like unto thee? or to thy faithfulness round about thee?

⁹Thou rulest the raging of the sea: when the waves thereof arise, thou stillest them.

¹⁰Thou hast broken Rahab in pieces, as one that is slain; thou hast scattered thine enemies with thy strong arm.

¹¹The heavens *are* thine, the earth also *is* thine: *as for* the world and the fulness thereof, thou hast founded them.

¹²The north and the south thou hast created them: Tabor and Hermon shall rejoice in thy name.

¹³Thou hast a mighty arm: strong is thy hand, *and* high is thy right hand.

¹⁴Justice and judgment *are* the habitation of thy throne: mercy and truth shall go before thy face.

¹⁵Blessed *is* the people that know the joyful sound: they shall walk, O LORD, in the light of thy countenance.

¹⁶In thy name shall they rejoice all the day: and in thy righteousness shall they be exalted.

¹⁷For thou *art* the glory of their strength: and in thy favour our horn shall be exalted.

¹⁸For the LORD *is* our defence; and the Holy One of Israel *is* our king.

¹⁹Then thou spakest in vision to thy holy one, and saidst, I have laid help upon *one that is* mighty; I have exalted *one* chosen out of the people.

²⁰I have found David my servant; with my holy oil have I anointed him:

²¹With whom my hand shall be established: mine arm also shall strengthen him.

²²The enemy shall not exact upon him; nor the son of wickedness afflict him.

²³And I will beat down his foes before his face, and plague them that hate him.

²⁴But my faithfulness and my mercy *shall be* with him: and in my name shall his horn be exalted.

²⁵I will set his hand also in the sea, and his right hand in the rivers.

²⁶He shall cry unto me, Thou *art* my father, my God, and the rock of my salvation.

²⁷Also I will make him *my* firstborn, higher than the kings of the earth.

²⁸My mercy will I keep for him for evermore, and my covenant shall stand fast with him.

²⁹His seed also will I make *to endure* for ever, and his throne as the days of heaven.

³⁰If his children forsake my law, and walk not in my judgments;

³¹If they break my statutes, and keep not my commandments;

³²Then will I visit their transgression with the rod, and their iniquity with stripes.

³³Nevertheless my lovingkindness will I not utterly take from him, nor suffer my faithfulness to fail.

³⁴My covenant will I not break, nor alter the thing that is gone out of my lips.

³⁵Once have I sworn by my holiness that I will not lie unto David.

³⁶His seed shall endure for ever, and his throne as the sun before me.

³⁷It shall be established for ever as the moon, and *as* a faithful witness in heaven. Selah.

³⁸But thou hast cast off and abhorred, thou hast been wroth with thine anointed.

³⁹Thou hast made void the covenant of thy servant: thou hast profaned his crown *by casting it* to the ground.

⁴⁰Thou hast broken down all his hedges; thou hast brought his strong holds to ruin.

⁴¹All that pass by the way spoil him: he is a reproach to his neighbours.

⁴²Thou hast set up the right hand of his adversaries; thou hast made all his enemies to rejoice.

⁴³Thou hast also turned the edge of his sword, and hast not made him to stand in the battle.

⁴⁴Thou hast made his glory to cease, and cast his throne down to the ground.

⁴⁵The days of his youth hast thou shortened: thou hast covered him with shame. Selah.

⁴⁶How long, LORD? wilt thou hide thyself for ever? shall thy wrath burn like fire?

⁴⁷Remember how short my time is: wherefore hast thou made all men in vain?

⁴⁸What man *is he that* liveth, and shall not see death? shall he deliver his soul from the hand of the grave? Selah.

⁴⁹Lord, where *are* thy former lovingkindnesses, *which* thou swarest unto David in thy truth?

⁵⁰Remember, Lord, the reproach of thy servants; *how* I do bear in my bosom *the reproach of* all the mighty people;

⁵¹Wherewith thine enemies have reproached, O LORD; wherewith they have reproached the footsteps of thine anointed.

⁵²Blessed *be* the LORD for evermore. Amen, and Amen.

Book IV

Psalm 90

A Prayer of Moses the man of God.

¹LORD, thou hast been our dwelling place in all generations.

²Before the mountains were brought forth, or ever thou hadst formed the earth and the world, even from everlasting to everlasting, thou *art* God.

³Thou turnest man to destruction; and sayest, Return, ye children of men.

⁴For a thousand years in thy sight *are but* as yesterday when it is past, and *as* a watch in the night.

⁵Thou carriest them away as with a flood; they are *as* a sleep: in the morning *they are* like grass *which* groweth up.

⁶In the morning it flourisheth, and groweth up; in the evening it is cut down, and withereth.

⁷For we are consumed by thine anger, and by thy wrath are we troubled.

⁸Thou hast set our iniquities before thee, our secret *sins* in the light of thy countenance.

⁹For all our days are passed away in thy wrath: we spend our years as a tale *that is told.*

¹⁰The days of our years *are* threescore years and ten; and if by reason of strength *they be* fourscore years, yet *is* their strength labour and sorrow; for it is soon cut off, and we fly away.

¹¹Who knoweth the power of thine anger? even according to thy fear, *so is* thy wrath.

¹²So teach *us* to number our days, that we may apply *our* hearts unto wisdom.

¹³Return, O LORD, how long? and let it repent thee concerning thy servants.

¹⁴O satisfy us early with thy mercy; that we may rejoice and be glad all our days.

¹⁵Make us glad according to the days *wherein* thou hast afflicted us, *and* the years *wherein* we have seen evil.

¹⁶Let thy work appear unto thy servants, and thy glory unto their children.

¹⁷And let the beauty of the LORD our God be upon us: and establish thou the work of our hands upon us; yea, the work of our hands establish thou it.

Psalm 91

¹He that dwelleth in the secret place of the most High shall abide under the shadow of the Almighty.

²I will say of the LORD, *He is* my refuge and my fortress: my God; in him will I trust.

³Surely he shall deliver thee from the snare of the fowler, *and* from the noisome pestilence.

⁴He shall cover thee with his feathers, and under his wings shalt thou trust: his truth *shall be thy* shield and buckler.

⁵Thou shalt not be afraid for the terror by night; *nor* for the arrow *that* flieth by day;

⁶*Nor* for the pestilence *that* walketh in darkness; *nor* for the destruction *that* wasteth at noonday.

⁷A thousand shall fall at thy side, and ten thousand at thy right hand; *but* it shall not come nigh thee.

⁸Only with thine eyes shalt thou behold and see the reward of the wicked.

⁹Because thou hast made the LORD, *which is* my refuge, *even* the most High, thy habitation;

¹⁰There shall no evil befall thee, neither shall any plague come nigh thy dwelling.

¹¹For he shall give his angels charge over thee, to keep thee in all thy ways.

¹²They shall bear thee up in *their* hands, lest thou dash thy foot against a stone.

¹³Thou shalt tread upon the lion and adder: the young lion and the dragon shalt thou trample under feet.

¹⁴Because he hath set his love upon me, therefore will I deliver him: I will set him on high, because he hath known my name.

¹⁵He shall call upon me, and I will answer him: I *will be* with him in trouble; I will deliver him, and honour him.

¹⁶With long life will I satisfy him, and shew him my salvation.

Psalm 92

A Psalm *or* Song for the sabbath day.

¹*It is a* good *thing* to give thanks unto the LORD, and to sing praises unto thy name, O most High:

²To shew forth thy lovingkindness in the morning, and thy faithfulness every night,

³Upon an instrument of ten strings, and upon the psaltery; upon the harp with a solemn sound.

⁴For thou, LORD, hast made me glad through thy work: I will triumph in the works of thy hands.

⁵O LORD, how great are thy works! *and* thy thoughts are very deep.

⁶A brutish man knoweth not; neither doth a fool understand this.

⁷When the wicked spring as the grass, and when all the workers of iniquity do flourish; *it is* that they shall be destroyed for ever:

⁸But thou, LORD, *art most* high for evermore.

⁹For, lo, thine enemies, O LORD, for, lo, thine enemies shall perish; all the workers of iniquity shall be scattered.

¹⁰But my horn shalt thou exalt like *the horn of* an unicorn: I shall be anointed with fresh oil.

¹¹Mine eye also shall see *my desire* on mine enemies, *and* mine ears shall hear *my desire* of the wicked that rise up against me.

¹²The righteous shall flourish like the palm tree: he shall grow like a cedar in Lebanon.

¹³Those that be planted in the house of the LORD shall flourish in the courts of our God.

¹⁴They shall still bring forth fruit in old age; they shall be fat and flourishing;

¹⁵To shew that the LORD *is* upright: *he is* my rock, and *there is* no unrighteousness in him.

Psalm 93

¹The LORD reigneth, he is clothed with majesty; the LORD is clothed with strength, *wherewith* he hath girded himself: the world also is stablished, that it cannot be moved.
²Thy throne *is* established of old: thou *art* from everlasting.
³The floods have lifted up, O LORD, the floods have lifted up their voice; the floods lift up their waves.

⁴The LORD on high *is* mightier than the noise of many waters, *yea, than* the mighty waves of the sea.
⁵Thy testimonies are very sure: holiness becometh thine house, O LORD, for ever.

Psalm 94

¹O LORD God, to whom vengeance belongeth; O God, to whom vengeance belongeth, shew thyself.
²Lift up thyself, thou judge of the earth: render a reward to the proud.
³LORD, how long shall the wicked, how long shall the wicked triumph?
⁴*How long* shall they utter *and* speak hard things? *and* all the workers of iniquity boast themselves?
⁵They break in pieces thy people, O LORD, and afflict thine heritage.
⁶They slay the widow and the stranger, and murder the fatherless.
⁷Yet they say, The LORD shall not see, neither shall the God of Jacob regard *it.*
⁸Understand, ye brutish among the people: and *ye* fools, when will ye be wise?
⁹He that planted the ear, shall he not hear? he that formed the eye, shall he not see?
¹⁰He that chastiseth the heathen, shall not he correct? he that teacheth man knowledge, *shall not he know?*
¹¹The LORD knoweth the thoughts of man, that they *are* vanity.
¹²Blessed *is* the man whom thou chastenest, O LORD, and teachest him out of thy law;
¹³That thou mayest give him rest from the days of adversity, until the pit be digged for the wicked.
¹⁴For the LORD will not cast off his people, neither will he forsake his inheritance.
¹⁵But judgment shall return unto righteousness: and all the upright in heart shall follow it.
¹⁶Who will rise up for me against the evildoers? *or* who will stand up for me against the workers of iniquity?
¹⁷Unless the LORD *had been* my help, my soul had almost dwelt in silence.

¹⁸When I said, My foot slippeth; thy mercy, O LORD, held me up.
¹⁹In the multitude of my thoughts within me thy comforts delight my soul.
²⁰Shall the throne of iniquity have fellowship with thee, which frameth mischief by a law?
²¹They gather themselves together against the soul of the righteous, and condemn the innocent blood.
²²But the LORD is my defence; and my God *is* the rock of my refuge.
²³And he shall bring upon them their own iniquity, and shall cut them off in their own wickedness; *yea,* the LORD our God shall cut them off.

Psalm 95

¹O come, let us sing unto the LORD: let us make a joyful noise to the rock of our salvation.
²Let us come before his presence with thanksgiving, and make a joyful noise unto him with psalms.
³For the LORD *is* a great God, and a great King above all gods.
⁴In his hand *are* the deep places of the earth: the strength of the hills *is* his also.
⁵The sea *is* his, and he made it: and his hands formed the dry *land.*
⁶O come, let us worship and bow down: let us kneel before the LORD our maker.
⁷For he *is* our God; and we *are* the people of his pasture, and the sheep of his hand. To day if ye will hear his voice,
⁸Harden not your heart, as in the provocation, *and as in* the day of temptation in the wilderness:
⁹When your fathers tempted me, proved me, and saw my work.
¹⁰Forty years long was I grieved with *this* generation, and said, It *is* a people that do err in their heart, and they have not known my ways:
¹¹Unto whom I sware in my wrath that they should not enter into my rest.

Psalm 96

¹O sing unto the LORD a new song: sing unto the LORD, all the earth.
²Sing unto the LORD, bless his name; shew forth his salvation from day to day.
³Declare his glory among the heathen, his wonders among all people.
⁴For the LORD *is* great, and greatly to be praised: he *is* to be feared above all gods.
⁵For all the gods of the nations *are* idols: but the LORD made the heavens.
⁶Honour and majesty *are* before him: strength and beauty *are* in his sanctuary.
⁷Give unto the LORD, O ye kindreds of the people, give unto the LORD glory and strength.

⁸Give unto the LORD the glory *due unto* his name: bring an offering, and come into his courts.

⁹O worship the LORD in the beauty of holiness: fear before him, all the earth.

¹⁰Say among the heathen *that* the LORD reigneth: the world also shall be established that it shall not be moved: he shall judge the people righteously.

¹¹Let the heavens rejoice, and let the earth be glad; let the sea roar, and the fulness thereof.

¹²Let the field be joyful, and all that *is* therein: then shall all the trees of the wood rejoice

¹³Before the LORD: for he cometh, for he cometh to judge the earth: he shall judge the world with righteousness, and the people with his truth.

Psalm 97

¹The LORD reigneth; let the earth rejoice; let the multitude of isles be glad *thereof.*

²Clouds and darkness *are* round about him: righteousness and judgment *are* the habitation of his throne.

³A fire goeth before him, and burneth up his enemies round about.

⁴His lightnings enlightened the world: the earth saw, and trembled.

⁵The hills melted like wax at the presence of the LORD, at the presence of the Lord of the whole earth.

⁶The heavens declare his righteousness, and all the people see his glory.

⁷Confounded be all they that serve graven images, that boast themselves of idols: worship him, all *ye* gods.

⁸Zion heard, and was glad; and the daughters of Judah rejoiced because of thy judgments, O LORD.

⁹For thou, LORD, *art* high above all the earth: thou art exalted far above all gods.

¹⁰Ye that love the LORD, hate evil: he preserveth the souls of his saints; he delivereth them out of the hand of the wicked.

¹¹Light is sown for the righteous, and gladness for the upright in heart.

¹²Rejoice in the LORD, ye righteous; and give thanks at the remembrance of his holiness.

Psalm 98

A Psalm.

¹O sing unto the LORD a new song; for he hath done marvellous things: his right hand, and his holy arm, hath gotten him the victory.

²The LORD hath made known his salvation: his righteousness hath he openly shewed in the sight of the heathen.

³He hath remembered his mercy and his truth toward the house of Israel: all the ends of the earth have seen the salvation of our God.

⁴Make a joyful noise unto the LORD, all the earth: make a loud noise, and rejoice, and sing praise.

⁵Sing unto the LORD with the harp; with the harp, and the voice of a psalm.

⁶With trumpets and sound of cornet make a joyful noise before the LORD, the King.

⁷Let the sea roar, and the fulness thereof; the world, and they that dwell therein.

⁸Let the floods clap *their* hands: let the hills be joyful together

⁹Before the LORD; for he cometh to judge the earth: with righteousness shall he judge the world, and the people with equity.

Psalm 99

¹The LORD reigneth; let the people tremble: he sitteth *between* the cherubims; let the earth be moved.

²The LORD *is* great in Zion; and he *is* high above all the people.

³Let them praise thy great and terrible name; *for* it *is* holy.

⁴The king's strength also loveth judgment; thou dost establish equity, thou executest judgment and righteousness in Jacob.

⁵Exalt ye the LORD our God, and worship at his footstool; *for* he *is* holy.

⁶Moses and Aaron among his priests, and Samuel among them that call upon his name; they called upon the LORD, and he answered them.

⁷He spake unto them in the cloudy pillar: they kept his testimonies, and the ordinance *that* he gave them.

⁸Thou answeredst them, O LORD our God: thou wast a God that forgavest them, though thou tookest vengeance of their inventions.

⁹Exalt the LORD our God, and worship at his holy hill; for the LORD our God *is* holy.

Psalm 100

A Psalm of praise.

¹Make a joyful noise unto the LORD, all ye lands.
²Serve the LORD with gladness: come before his presence with singing.
³Know ye that the LORD he *is* God: *it is* he *that* hath made us, and not we ourselves; *we are* his people, and the sheep of his pasture.
⁴Enter into his gates with thanksgiving, *and* into his courts with praise: be thankful unto him, *and* bless his name.
⁵For the LORD *is* good; his mercy *is* everlasting; and his truth *endureth* to all generations.

Psalm 101

A Psalm of David.

¹I will sing of mercy and judgment: unto thee, O LORD, will I sing.
²I will behave myself wisely in a perfect way. O when wilt thou come unto me? I will walk within my house with a perfect heart.
³I will set no wicked thing before mine eyes: I hate the work of them that turn aside; *it* shall not cleave to me.
⁴A froward heart shall depart from me: I will not know a wicked *person.*
⁵Whoso privily slandereth his neighbour, him will I cut off: him that hath an high look and a proud heart will not I suffer.
⁶Mine eyes *shall be* upon the faithful of the land, that they may dwell with me: he that walketh in a perfect way, he shall serve me.
⁷He that worketh deceit shall not dwell within my house: he that telleth lies shall not tarry in my sight.
⁸I will early destroy all the wicked of the land; that I may cut off all wicked doers from the city of the LORD.

Psalm 102

A Prayer of the afflicted, when he is overwhelmed, and poureth out his complaint before the LORD.

¹Hear my prayer, O LORD, and let my cry come unto thee.

²Hide not thy face from me in the day *when* I am in trouble; incline thine ear unto me: in the day *when* I call answer me speedily.

³For my days are consumed like smoke, and my bones are burned as an hearth.

⁴My heart is smitten, and withered like grass; so that I forget to eat my bread.

⁵By reason of the voice of my groaning my bones cleave to my skin.

⁶I am like a pelican of the wilderness: I am like an owl of the desert.

⁷I watch, and am as a sparrow alone upon the house top.

⁸Mine enemies reproach me all the day; *and* they that are mad against me are sworn against me.

⁹For I have eaten ashes like bread, and mingled my drink with weeping,

¹⁰Because of thine indignation and thy wrath: for thou hast lifted me up, and cast me down.

¹¹My days *are* like a shadow that declineth; and I am withered like grass.

¹²But thou, O LORD, shalt endure for ever; and thy remembrance unto all generations.

¹³Thou shalt arise, *and* have mercy upon Zion: for the time to favour her, yea, the set time, is come.

¹⁴For thy servants take pleasure in her stones, and favour the dust thereof.

¹⁵So the heathen shall fear the name of the LORD, and all the kings of the earth thy glory.

¹⁶When the LORD shall build up Zion, he shall appear in his glory.

¹⁷He will regard the prayer of the destitute, and not despise their prayer.

¹⁸This shall be written for the generation to come: and the people which shall be created shall praise the LORD.

¹⁹For he hath looked down from the height of his sanctuary; from heaven did the LORD behold the earth;

²⁰To hear the groaning of the prisoner; to loose those that are appointed to death;

²¹To declare the name of the LORD in Zion, and his praise in Jerusalem;

²²When the people are gathered together, and the kingdoms, to serve the LORD.

²³He weakened my strength in the way; he shortened my days.

²⁴I said, O my God, take me not away in the midst of my days: thy years *are* throughout all generations.

²⁵Of old hast thou laid the foundation of the earth: and the heavens *are* the work of thy hands.

²⁶They shall perish, but thou shalt endure: yea, all of them shall wax old like a garment; as a vesture shalt thou change them, and they shall be changed:

²⁷But thou *art* the same, and thy years shall have no end.

²⁸The children of thy servants shall continue, and their seed shall be established before thee.

Psalm 103

A *Psalm* of David.

¹Bless the LORD, O my soul: and all that is within me, *bless* his holy name.

²Bless the LORD, O my soul, and forget not all his benefits:

³Who forgiveth all thine iniquities; who healeth all thy diseases;

⁴Who redeemeth thy life from destruction; who crowneth thee with lovingkindness and tender mercies;

⁵Who satisfieth thy mouth with good *things; so that* thy youth is renewed like the eagle's.

⁶The LORD executeth righteousness and judgment for all that are oppressed.

⁷He made known his ways unto Moses, his acts unto the children of Israel.

⁸The LORD *is* merciful and gracious, slow to anger, and plenteous in mercy.

⁹He will not always chide: neither will he keep *his anger* for ever.

¹⁰He hath not dealt with us after our sins; nor rewarded us according to our iniquities.

¹¹For as the heaven is high above the earth, *so* great is his mercy toward them that fear him.

¹²As far as the east is from the west, *so* far hath he removed our transgressions from us.

¹³Like as a father pitieth *his* children, *so* the LORD pitieth them that fear him.

¹⁴For he knoweth our frame; he remembereth that we *are* dust.

¹⁵*As for* man, his days *are* as grass: as a flower of the field, so he flourisheth.

¹⁶For the wind passeth over it, and it is gone; and the place thereof shall know it no more.

¹⁷But the mercy of the LORD *is* from everlasting to everlasting upon them that fear him, and his righteousness unto children's children;

¹⁸To such as keep his covenant, and to those that remember his commandments to do them.

¹⁹The LORD hath prepared his throne in the heavens; and his kingdom ruleth over all.

²⁰Bless the LORD, ye his angels, that excel in strength, that do his commandments, hearkening unto the voice of his word.

²¹Bless ye the LORD, all *ye* his hosts; *ye* ministers of his, that do his pleasure.

²²Bless the LORD, all his works in all places of his dominion: bless the LORD, O my soul.

Psalm 104

¹Bless the LORD, O my soul. O LORD my God, thou art very great; thou art clothed with honour and majesty.

²Who coverest *thyself* with light as *with* a garment: who stretchest out the heavens like a curtain:

³Who layeth the beams of his chambers in the waters: who maketh the clouds his chariot: who walketh upon the wings of the wind:

⁴Who maketh his angels spirits; his ministers a flaming fire:

⁵*Who* laid the foundations of the earth, *that* it should not be removed for ever.

⁶Thou coveredst it with the deep as *with* a garment: the waters stood above the mountains.

^{7}At thy rebuke they fled; at the voice of thy thunder they hasted away.

^{8}They go up by the mountains; they go down by the valleys unto the place which thou hast founded for them.

^{9}Thou hast set a bound that they may not pass over; that they turn not again to cover the earth.

^{10}He sendeth the springs into the valleys, *which* run among the hills.

^{11}They give drink to every beast of the field: the wild asses quench their thirst.

^{12}By them shall the fowls of the heaven have their habitation, *which* sing among the branches.

^{13}He watereth the hills from his chambers: the earth is satisfied with the fruit of thy works.

^{14}He causeth the grass to grow for the cattle, and herb for the service of man: that he may bring forth food out of the earth;

^{15}And wine *that* maketh glad the heart of man, *and* oil to make *his* face to shine, and bread *which* strengtheneth man's heart.

^{16}The trees of the LORD are full *of sap;* the cedars of Lebanon, which he hath planted;

^{17}Where the birds make their nests: *as for* the stork, the fir trees *are* her house.

^{18}The high hills *are* a refuge for the wild goats; *and* the rocks for the conies.

^{19}He appointed the moon for seasons: the sun knoweth his going down.

^{20}Thou makest darkness, and it is night: wherein all the beasts of the forest do creep *forth.*

^{21}The young lions roar after their prey, and seek their meat from God.

^{22}The sun ariseth, they gather themselves together, and lay them down in their dens.

^{23}Man goeth forth unto his work and to his labour until the evening.

^{24}O LORD, how manifold are thy works! in wisdom hast thou made them all: the earth is full of thy riches.

^{25}*So is* this great and wide sea, wherein *are* things creeping innumerable, both small and great beasts.

^{26}There go the ships: *there is* that leviathan, *whom* thou hast made to play therein.

^{27}These wait all upon thee; that thou mayest give *them* their meat in due season.

^{28}*That* thou givest them they gather: thou openest thine hand, they are filled with good.

^{29}Thou hidest thy face, they are troubled: thou takest away their breath, they die, and return to their dust.

^{30}Thou sendest forth thy spirit, they are created: and thou renewest the face of the earth.

^{31}The glory of the LORD shall endure for ever: the LORD shall rejoice in his works.

^{32}He looketh on the earth, and it trembleth: he toucheth the hills, and they smoke.

^{33}I will sing unto the LORD as long as I live: I will sing praise to my God while I have my being.

^{34}My meditation of him shall be sweet: I will be glad in the LORD.

^{35}Let the sinners be consumed out of the earth, and let the wicked be no more. Bless thou the LORD, O my soul. Praise ye the LORD.

Psalm 105

¹O give thanks unto the LORD; call upon his name: make known his deeds among the people.

²Sing unto him, sing psalms unto him: talk ye of all his wondrous works.

³Glory ye in his holy name: let the heart of them rejoice that seek the LORD.

⁴Seek the LORD, and his strength: seek his face evermore.

⁵Remember his marvellous works that he hath done; his wonders, and the judgments of his mouth;

⁶O ye seed of Abraham his servant, ye children of Jacob his chosen.

⁷He *is* the LORD our God: his judgments *are* in all the earth.

⁸He hath remembered his covenant for ever, the word *which* he commanded to a thousand generations.

⁹Which *covenant* he made with Abraham, and his oath unto Isaac;

¹⁰And confirmed the same unto Jacob for a law, *and* to Israel *for* an everlasting covenant:

¹¹Saying, Unto thee will I give the land of Canaan, the lot of your inheritance:

¹²When they were *but* a few men in number; yea, very few, and strangers in it.

¹³When they went from one nation to another, from *one* kingdom to another people;

¹⁴He suffered no man to do them wrong: yea, he reproved kings for their sakes;

¹⁵*Saying,* Touch not mine anointed, and do my prophets no harm.

¹⁶Moreover he called for a famine upon the land: he brake the whole staff of bread.

¹⁷He sent a man before them, *even* Joseph, *who* was sold for a servant:

¹⁸Whose feet they hurt with fetters: he was laid in iron:

¹⁹Until the time that his word came: the word of the LORD tried him.

²⁰The king sent and loosed him; *even* the ruler of the people, and let him go free.

²¹He made him lord of his house, and ruler of all his substance:

²²To bind his princes at his pleasure; and teach his senators wisdom.

²³Israel also came into Egypt; and Jacob sojourned in the land of Ham.

²⁴And he increased his people greatly; and made them stronger than their enemies.

²⁵He turned their heart to hate his people, to deal subtilly with his servants.

²⁶He sent Moses his servant; *and* Aaron whom he had chosen.

²⁷They shewed his signs among them, and wonders in the land of Ham.

²⁸He sent darkness, and made it dark; and they rebelled not against his word.

²⁹He turned their waters into blood, and slew their fish.

³⁰Their land brought forth frogs in abundance, in the chambers of their kings.

³¹He spake, and there came divers sorts of flies, *and* lice in all their coasts.

³²He gave them hail for rain, *and* flaming fire in their land.

³³He smote their vines also and their fig trees; and brake the trees of their coasts.

³⁴He spake, and the locusts came, and caterpillers, and that without number,

³⁵And did eat up all the herbs in their land, and devoured the fruit of their ground.

³⁶He smote also all the firstborn in their land, the chief of all their strength.

³⁷He brought them forth also with silver and gold: and *there was* not one feeble *person* among their tribes.

³⁸Egypt was glad when they departed: for the fear of them fell upon them.

³⁹He spread a cloud for a covering; and fire to give light in the night.

⁴⁰*The people* asked, and he brought quails, and satisfied them with the bread of heaven.

⁴¹He opened the rock, and the waters gushed out; they ran in the dry places *like* a river.

⁴²For he remembered his holy promise, *and* Abraham his servant.

⁴³And he brought forth his people with joy, *and* his chosen with gladness:

⁴⁴And gave them the lands of the heathen: and they inherited the labour of the people;

⁴⁵That they might observe his statutes, and keep his laws. Praise ye the LORD.

Psalm 106

¹Praise ye the LORD. O give thanks unto the LORD; for *he is* good: for his mercy *endureth* for ever.

²Who can utter the mighty acts of the LORD? *who* can shew forth all his praise?

³Blessed *are* they that keep judgment, *and* he that doeth righteousness at all times.

⁴Remember me, O LORD, with the favour *that thou bearest unto* thy people: O visit me with thy salvation;

⁵That I may see the good of thy chosen, that I may rejoice in the gladness of thy nation, that I may glory with thine inheritance.

⁶We have sinned with our fathers, we have committed iniquity, we have done wickedly.

⁷Our fathers understood not thy wonders in Egypt; they remembered not the multitude of thy mercies; but provoked *him* at the sea, *even* at the Red sea.

⁸Nevertheless he saved them for his name's sake, that he might make his mighty power to be known.

⁹He rebuked the Red sea also, and it was dried up: so he led them through the depths, as through the wilderness.

¹⁰And he saved them from the hand of him that hated *them,* and redeemed them from the hand of the enemy.

¹¹And the waters covered their enemies: there was not one of them left.

¹²Then believed they his words; they sang his praise.

¹³They soon forgat his works; they waited not for his counsel:

¹⁴But lusted exceedingly in the wilderness, and tempted God in the desert.

¹⁵And he gave them their request; but sent leanness into their soul.

¹⁶They envied Moses also in the camp, *and* Aaron the saint of the LORD.

¹⁷The earth opened and swallowed up Dathan, and covered the company of Abiram.

¹⁸And a fire was kindled in their company; the flame burned up the wicked.

¹⁹They made a calf in Horeb, and worshipped the molten image.

²⁰Thus they changed their glory into the similitude of an ox that eateth grass.

²¹They forgat God their saviour, which had done great things in Egypt;

²²Wondrous works in the land of Ham, *and* terrible things by the Red sea.

²³Therefore he said that he would destroy them, had not Moses his chosen stood before him in the breach, to turn away his wrath, lest he should destroy *them.*

²⁴Yea, they despised the pleasant land, they believed not his word:

²⁵But murmured in their tents, *and* hearkened not unto the voice of the LORD.

²⁶Therefore he lifted up his hand against them, to overthrow them in the wilderness:

²⁷To overthrow their seed also among the nations, and to scatter them in the lands.

²⁸They joined themselves also unto Baal-peor, and ate the sacrifices of the dead.

²⁹Thus they provoked *him* to anger with their inventions: and the plague brake in upon them.

³⁰Then stood up Phinehas, and executed judgment: and *so* the plague was stayed.

³¹And that was counted unto him for righteousness unto all generations for evermore.

³²They angered *him* also at the waters of strife, so that it went ill with Moses for their sakes:

³³Because they provoked his spirit, so that he spake unadvisedly with his lips.

³⁴They did not destroy the nations, concerning whom the LORD commanded them:

³⁵But were mingled among the heathen, and learned their works.

³⁶And they served their idols: which were a snare unto them.

³⁷Yea, they sacrificed their sons and their daughters unto devils,

³⁸And shed innocent blood, *even* the blood of their sons and of their daughters, whom they sacrificed unto the idols of Canaan: and the land was polluted with blood.

³⁹Thus were they defiled with their own works, and went a whoring with their own inventions.

⁴⁰Therefore was the wrath of the LORD kindled against his people, insomuch that he abhorred his own inheritance.

⁴¹And he gave them into the hand of the heathen; and they that hated them ruled over them.

⁴²Their enemies also oppressed them, and they were brought into subjection under their hand.

⁴³Many times did he deliver them; but they provoked *him* with their counsel, and were brought low for their iniquity.

⁴⁴Nevertheless he regarded their affliction, when he heard their cry:

⁴⁵And he remembered for them his covenant, and repented according to the multitude of his mercies.

⁴⁶He made them also to be pitied of all those that carried them captives.

⁴⁷Save us, O LORD our God, and gather us from among the heathen, to give thanks unto thy holy name, *and* to triumph in thy praise.

⁴⁸Blessed *be* the Lord God of Israel from everlasting to everlasting: and let all the people say, Amen. Praise ye the LORD.

Book V

Psalm 107

[1]O give thanks unto the LORD, for *he is* good: for his mercy *endureth* for ever.

[2]Let the redeemed of the LORD say so, whom he hath redeemed from the hand of the enemy;

[3]And gathered them out of the lands, from the east, and from the west, from the north, and from the south.

[4]They wandered in the wilderness in a solitary way; they found no city to dwell in.

[5]Hungry and thirsty, their soul fainted in them.

[6]Then they cried unto the LORD in their trouble, *and* he delivered them out of their distresses.

[7]And he led them forth by the right way, that they might go to a city of habitation.

[8]Oh that *men* would praise the LORD *for* his goodness, and *for* his wonderful works to the children of men!

[9]For he satisfieth the longing soul, and filleth the hungry soul with goodness.

[10]Such as sit in darkness and in the shadow of death, *being* bound in affliction and iron;

[11]Because they rebelled against the words of God, and contemned the counsel of the most High:

[12]Therefore he brought down their heart with labour; they fell down, and *there was* none to help.

[13]Then they cried unto the LORD in their trouble, *and* he saved them out of their distresses.

[14]He brought them out of darkness and the shadow of death, and brake their bands in sunder.

[15]Oh that *men* would praise the LORD *for* his goodness, and *for* his wonderful works to the children of men!

[16]For he hath broken the gates of brass, and cut the bars of iron in sunder.

[17]Fools because of their transgression, and because of their iniquities, are afflicted.

[18]Their soul abhorreth all manner of meat; and they draw near unto the gates of death.

[19]Then they cry unto the LORD in their trouble, *and* he saveth them out of their distresses.

[20]He sent his word, and healed them, and delivered *them* from their destructions.

[21]Oh that *men* would praise the LORD *for* his goodness, and *for* his wonderful works to the children of men!

[22]And let them sacrifice the sacrifices of thanksgiving, and declare his works with rejoicing.

[23]They that go down to the sea in ships, that do business in great waters;

[24]These see the works of the LORD, and his wonders in the deep.

[25]For he commandeth, and raiseth the stormy wind, which lifteth up the waves thereof.

[26]They mount up to the heaven, they go down again to the depths: their soul is melted because of trouble.

[27]They reel to and fro, and stagger like a drunken man, and are at their wit's end.

[28]Then they cry unto the LORD in their trouble, and he bringeth them out of their distresses.

²⁹He maketh the storm a calm, so that the waves thereof are still.

³⁰Then are they glad because they be quiet; so he bringeth them unto their desired haven.

³¹Oh that *men* would praise the LORD *for* his goodness, and *for* his wonderful works to the children of men!

³²Let them exalt him also in the congregation of the people, and praise him in the assembly of the elders.

³³He turneth rivers into a wilderness, and the watersprings into dry ground;

³⁴A fruitful land into barrenness, for the wickedness of them that dwell therein.

³⁵He turneth the wilderness into a standing water, and dry ground into watersprings.

³⁶And there he maketh the hungry to dwell, that they may prepare a city for habitation;

³⁷And sow the fields, and plant vineyards, which may yield fruits of increase.

³⁸He blesseth them also, so that they are multiplied greatly; and suffereth not their cattle to decrease.

³⁹Again, they are minished and brought low through oppression, affliction, and sorrow.

⁴⁰He poureth contempt upon princes, and causeth them to wander in the wilderness, *where there is* no way.

⁴¹Yet setteth he the poor on high from affliction, and maketh *him* families like a flock.

⁴²The righteous shall see *it,* and rejoice: and all iniquity shall stop her mouth.

⁴³Whoso *is* wise, and will observe these *things,* even they shall understand the lovingkindness of the LORD.

Psalm 108

A Song *or* Psalm of David.

¹O God, my heart is fixed; I will sing and give praise, even with my glory.

²Awake, psaltery and harp: I *myself* will awake early.

³I will praise thee, O LORD, among the people: and I will sing praises unto thee among the nations.

⁴For thy mercy *is* great above the heavens: and thy truth *reacheth* unto the clouds.

⁵Be thou exalted, O God, above the heavens: and thy glory above all the earth;

⁶That thy beloved may be delivered: save *with* thy right hand, and answer me.

⁷God hath spoken in his holiness; I will rejoice, I will divide Shechem, and mete out the valley of Succoth.

⁸Gilead *is* mine; Manasseh *is* mine; Ephraim also *is* the strength of mine head; Judah *is* my lawgiver;

⁹Moab *is* my washpot; over Edom will I cast out my shoe; over Philistia will I triumph.

¹⁰Who will bring me into the strong city? who will lead me into Edom?

¹¹*Wilt* not *thou,* O God, *who* hast cast us off? and wilt not thou, O God, go forth with our hosts?

¹²Give us help from trouble: for vain *is* the help of man.

¹³Through God we shall do valiantly: for he *it is that* shall tread down our enemies.

Psalm 109

To the chief Musician, A Psalm of David.

¹Hold not thy peace, O God of my praise;

²For the mouth of the wicked and the mouth of the deceitful are opened against me: they have spoken against me with a lying tongue.

³They compassed me about also with words of hatred; and fought against me without a cause.

⁴For my love they are my adversaries: but I *give myself unto* prayer.

⁵And they have rewarded me evil for good, and hatred for my love.

⁶Set thou a wicked man over him: and let Satan stand at his right hand.

⁷When he shall be judged, let him be condemned: and let his prayer become sin.

⁸Let his days be few; *and* let another take his office.

⁹Let his children be fatherless, and his wife a widow.

¹⁰Let his children be continually vagabonds, and beg: let them seek *their bread* also out of their desolate places.

¹¹Let the extortioner catch all that he hath; and let the strangers spoil his labour.

¹²Let there be none to extend mercy unto him: neither let there be any to favour his fatherless children.

¹³Let his posterity be cut off; *and* in the generation following let their name be blotted out.

¹⁴Let the iniquity of his fathers be remembered with the LORD; and let not the sin of his mother be blotted out.

¹⁵Let them be before the LORD continually, that he may cut off the memory of them from the earth.

¹⁶Because that he remembered not to shew mercy, but persecuted the poor and needy man, that he might even slay the broken in heart.

¹⁷As he loved cursing, so let it come unto him: as he delighted not in blessing, so let it be far from him.

¹⁸As he clothed himself with cursing like as with his garment, so let it come into his bowels like water, and like oil into his bones.

¹⁹Let it be unto him as the garment *which* covereth him, and for a girdle wherewith he is girded continually.

²⁰*Let* this *be* the reward of mine adversaries from the LORD, and of them that speak evil against my soul.

²¹But do thou for me, O GOD the Lord, for thy name's sake: because thy mercy *is* good, deliver thou me.

²²For I *am* poor and needy, and my heart is wounded within me.

²³I am gone like the shadow when it declineth: I am tossed up and down as the locust.

²⁴My knees are weak through fasting; and my flesh faileth of fatness.

²⁵I became also a reproach unto them: *when* they looked upon me they shaked their heads.

²⁶Help me, O LORD my God: O save me according to thy mercy:

²⁷That they may know that this *is* thy hand; *that* thou, LORD, hast done it.

²⁸Let them curse, but bless thou: when they arise, let them be ashamed; but let thy servant rejoice.

²⁹Let mine adversaries be clothed with shame, and let them cover themselves with their own confusion, as with a mantle.

³⁰I will greatly praise the LORD with my mouth; yea, I will praise him among the multitude.

³¹For he shall stand at the right hand of the poor, to save *him* from those that condemn his soul.

Psalm 110

A Psalm of David.

¹The LORD said unto my Lord, Sit thou at my right hand, until I make thine enemies thy footstool.

²The LORD shall send the rod of thy strength out of Zion: rule thou in the midst of thine enemies.

³Thy people *shall be* willing in the day of thy power, in the beauties of holiness from the womb of the morning: thou hast the dew of thy youth.

⁴The LORD hath sworn, and will not repent, Thou *art* a priest for ever after the order of Melchizedek.

⁵The Lord at thy right hand shall strike through kings in the day of his wrath.

⁶He shall judge among the heathen, he shall fill *the places* with the dead bodies; he shall wound the heads over many countries.

⁷He shall drink of the brook in the way: therefore shall he lift up the head.

Psalm 111

[1]Praise ye the LORD. I will praise the LORD with *my* whole heart, in the assembly of the upright, and *in* the congregation.

[2]The works of the LORD *are* great, sought out of all them that have pleasure therein.

[3]His work *is* honourable and glorious: and his righteousness endureth for ever.

[4]He hath made his wonderful works to be remembered: the LORD *is* gracious and full of compassion.

[5]He hath given meat unto them that fear him: he will ever be mindful of his covenant.

[6]He hath shewed his people the power of his works, that he may give them the heritage of the heathen.

[7]The works of his hands *are* verity and judgment; all his commandments *are* sure.

[8]They stand fast for ever and ever, *and are* done in truth and uprightness.

[9]He sent redemption unto his people: he hath commanded his covenant for ever: holy and reverend *is* his name.

[10]The fear of the LORD *is* the beginning of wisdom: a good understanding have all they that do *his commandments:* his praise endureth for ever.

Psalm 112

[1]Praise ye the LORD. Blessed *is* the man *that* feareth the LORD, *that* delighteth greatly in his commandments.

[2]His seed shall be mighty upon earth: the generation of the upright shall be blessed.

[3]Wealth and riches *shall be* in his house: and his righteousness endureth for ever.

[4]Unto the upright there ariseth light in the darkness: *he is* gracious, and full of compassion, and righteous.

[5]A good man sheweth favour, and lendeth: he will guide his affairs with discretion.

[6]Surely he shall not be moved for ever: the righteous shall be in everlasting remembrance.

[7]He shall not be afraid of evil tidings: his heart is fixed, trusting in the LORD.

[8]His heart *is* established, he shall not be afraid, until he see *his desire* upon his enemies.

[9]He hath dispersed, he hath given to the poor; his righteousness endureth for ever; his horn shall be exalted with honour.

[10]The wicked shall see *it,* and be grieved; he shall gnash with his teeth, and melt away: the desire of the wicked shall perish.

Psalm 113

¹Praise ye the LORD. Praise, O ye servants of the LORD, praise the name of the LORD.
²Blessed be the name of the LORD from this time forth and for evermore.
³From the rising of the sun unto the going down of the same the LORD'S name *is* to be praised.
⁴The LORD *is* high above all nations, *and* his glory above the heavens.
⁵Who *is* like unto the LORD our God, who dwelleth on high,
⁶Who humbleth *himself* to behold *the things that are* in heaven, and in the earth!
⁷He raiseth up the poor out of the dust, *and* lifteth the needy out of the dunghill;
⁸That he may set *him* with princes, *even* with the princes of his people.
⁹He maketh the barren woman to keep house, *and to be* a joyful mother of children. Praise ye the LORD.

Psalm 114

¹When Israel went out of Egypt, the house of Jacob from a people of strange language;
²Judah was his sanctuary, *and* Israel his dominion.
³The sea saw *it,* and fled: Jordan was driven back.
⁴The mountains skipped like rams, *and* the little hills like lambs.
⁵What *ailed* thee, O thou sea, that thou fleddest? thou Jordan, *that* thou wast driven back?
⁶Ye mountains, *that* ye skipped like rams; *and* ye little hills, like lambs?
⁷Tremble, thou earth, at the presence of the Lord, at the presence of the God of Jacob;
⁸Which turned the rock *into* a standing water, the flint into a fountain of waters.

Psalm 115

¹Not unto us, O LORD, not unto us, but unto thy name give glory, for thy mercy, *and* for thy truth's sake.
²Wherefore should the heathen say, Where *is* now their God?
³But our God *is* in the heavens: he hath done whatsoever he hath pleased.
⁴Their idols *are* silver and gold, the work of men's hands.
⁵They have mouths, but they speak not: eyes have they, but they see not:
⁶They have ears, but they hear not: noses have they, but they smell not:
⁷They have hands, but they handle not: feet have they, but they walk not: neither speak they through their throat.
⁸They that make them are like unto them; *so is* every one that trusteth in them.

⁹O Israel, trust thou in the LORD: he *is* their help and their shield.

¹⁰O house of Aaron, trust in the LORD: he *is* their help and their shield.

¹¹Ye that fear the LORD, trust in the LORD: he *is* their help and their shield.

¹²The LORD hath been mindful of us: he will bless *us;* he will bless the house of Israel; he will bless the house of Aaron.

¹³He will bless them that fear the LORD, *both* small and great.

¹⁴The LORD shall increase you more and more, you and your children.

¹⁵Ye *are* blessed of the LORD which made heaven and earth.

¹⁶The heaven, *even* the heavens, *are* the LORD'S: but the earth hath he given to the children of men.

¹⁷The dead praise not the LORD, neither any that go down into silence.

¹⁸But we will bless the LORD from this time forth and for evermore. Praise the LORD.

Psalm 116

¹I love the LORD, because he hath heard my voice *and* my supplications.

²Because he hath inclined his ear unto me, therefore will I call upon *him* as long as I live.

³The sorrows of death compassed me, and the pains of hell gat hold upon me: I found trouble and sorrow.

⁴Then called I upon the name of the LORD; O LORD, I beseech thee, deliver my soul.

⁵Gracious *is* the LORD, and righteous; yea, our God *is* merciful.

⁶The LORD preserveth the simple: I was brought low, and he helped me.

⁷Return unto thy rest, O my soul; for the LORD hath dealt bountifully with thee.

⁸For thou hast delivered my soul from death, mine eyes from tears, *and* my feet from falling.

⁹I will walk before the LORD in the land of the living.

¹⁰I believed, therefore have I spoken: I was greatly afflicted:

¹¹I said in my haste, All men *are* liars.

¹²What shall I render unto the LORD *for* all his benefits toward me?

¹³I will take the cup of salvation, and call upon the name of the LORD.

¹⁴I will pay my vows unto the LORD now in the presence of all his people.

¹⁵Precious in the sight of the LORD *is* the death of his saints.

¹⁶O LORD, truly I *am* thy servant; I *am* thy servant, *and* the son of thine handmaid: thou hast loosed my bonds.

¹⁷I will offer to thee the sacrifice of thanksgiving, and will call upon the name of the LORD.

¹⁸I will pay my vows unto the LORD now in the presence of all his people,

¹⁹In the courts of the LORD'S house, in the midst of thee, O Jerusalem. Praise ye the LORD.

Psalm 117

¹O praise the LORD, all ye nations: praise him, all ye people.

²For his merciful kindness is great toward us: and the truth of the LORD *endureth* for ever. Praise ye the LORD.

Psalm 118

¹O give thanks unto the LORD; for *he is* good: because his mercy *endureth* for ever.

²Let Israel now say, that his mercy *endureth* for ever.

³Let the house of Aaron now say, that his mercy *endureth* for ever.

⁴Let them now that fear the LORD say, that his mercy *endureth* for ever.

⁵I called upon the LORD in distress: the LORD answered me, *and set me* in a large place.

⁶The LORD *is* on my side; I will not fear: what can man do unto me?

⁷The LORD taketh my part with them that help me: therefore shall I see *my desire* upon them that hate me.

⁸*It is* better to trust in the LORD than to put confidence in man.

⁹*It is* better to trust in the LORD than to put confidence in princes.

¹⁰All nations compassed me about: but in the name of the LORD will I destroy them.

¹¹They compassed me about; yea, they compassed me about: but in the name of the LORD I will destroy them.

¹²They compassed me about like bees; they are quenched as the fire of thorns: for in the name of the LORD I will destroy them.

¹³Thou hast thrust sore at me that I might fall: but the LORD helped me.

¹⁴The LORD *is* my strength and song, and is become my salvation.

¹⁵The voice of rejoicing and salvation *is* in the tabernacles of the righteous: the right hand of the LORD doeth valiantly.

¹⁶The right hand of the LORD is exalted: the right hand of the LORD doeth valiantly.

¹⁷I shall not die, but live, and declare the works of the LORD.

¹⁸The LORD hath chastened me sore: but he hath not given me over unto death.

¹⁹Open to me the gates of righteousness: I will go into them, *and* I will praise the LORD:

²⁰This gate of the LORD, into which the righteous shall enter.

²¹I will praise thee: for thou hast heard me, and art become my salvation.

²²The stone *which* the builders refused is become the head *stone* of the corner.

²³This is the LORD'S doing; it *is* marvellous in our eyes.

²⁴This *is* the day *which* the LORD hath made; we will rejoice and be glad in it.

²⁵Save now, I beseech thee, O LORD: O LORD, I beseech thee, send now prosperity.

²⁶Blessed *be* he that cometh in the name of the LORD: we have blessed you out of the house of the LORD.

²⁷God *is* the LORD, which hath shewed us light: bind the sacrifice with cords, *even* unto the horns of the altar.

²⁸Thou *art* my God, and I will praise thee: *thou art* my God, I will exalt thee.

²⁹O give thanks unto the LORD; for *he is* good: for his mercy *endureth* for ever.

Psalm 119

ALEPH.

¹Blessed *are* the undefiled in the way, who walk in the law of the LORD.

²Blessed *are* they that keep his testimonies, *and that* seek him with the whole heart.

³They also do no iniquity: they walk in his ways.

⁴Thou hast commanded *us* to keep thy precepts diligently.

⁵O that my ways were directed to keep thy statutes!

⁶Then shall I not be ashamed, when I have respect unto all thy commandments.

⁷I will praise thee with uprightness of heart, when I shall have learned thy righteous judgments.

⁸I will keep thy statutes: O forsake me not utterly.

BETH.

⁹Wherewithal shall a young man cleanse his way? by taking heed *thereto* according to thy word.

¹⁰With my whole heart have I sought thee: O let me not wander from thy commandments.

¹¹Thy word have I hid in mine heart, that I might not sin against thee.

¹²Blessed *art* thou, O LORD: teach me thy statutes.

¹³With my lips have I declared all the judgments of thy mouth.

¹⁴I have rejoiced in the way of thy testimonies, as *much as* in all riches.

¹⁵I will meditate in thy precepts, and have respect unto thy ways.

¹⁶I will delight myself in thy statutes: I will not forget thy word.

GIMEL.

¹⁷Deal bountifully with thy servant, *that* I may live, and keep thy word.

¹⁸Open thou mine eyes, that I may behold wondrous things out of thy law.

¹⁹I *am* a stranger in the earth: hide not thy commandments from me.

²⁰My soul breaketh for the longing *that it hath* unto thy judgments at all times.

²¹Thou hast rebuked the proud *that are* cursed, which do err from thy commandments.

²²Remove from me reproach and contempt; for I have kept thy testimonies.

²³Princes also did sit *and* speak against me: *but* thy servant did meditate in thy statutes.

²⁴Thy testimonies also *are* my delight *and* my counsellors.

DALETH.

²⁵My soul cleaveth unto the dust: quicken thou me according to thy word.

²⁶I have declared my ways, and thou heardest me: teach me thy statutes.

²⁷Make me to understand the way of thy precepts: so shall I talk of thy wondrous works.

²⁸My soul melteth for heaviness: strengthen thou me according unto thy word.

²⁹Remove from me the way of lying: and grant me thy law graciously.

³⁰I have chosen the way of truth: thy judgments have I laid *before me.*

³¹I have stuck unto thy testimonies: O LORD, put me not to shame.

³²I will run the way of thy commandments, when thou shalt enlarge my heart.

HE.

³³Teach me, O LORD, the way of thy statutes; and I shall keep it *unto* the end.

³⁴Give me understanding, and I shall keep thy law; yea, I shall observe it with *my* whole heart.

³⁵Make me to go in the path of thy commandments; for therein do I delight.

³⁶Incline my heart unto thy testimonies, and not to covetousness.

³⁷Turn away mine eyes from beholding vanity; *and* quicken thou me in thy way.

³⁸Stablish thy word unto thy servant, who *is devoted* to thy fear.

³⁹Turn away my reproach which I fear: for thy judgments *are* good.

⁴⁰Behold, I have longed after thy precepts: quicken me in thy righteousness.

VAU.

⁴¹Let thy mercies come also unto me, O LORD, *even* thy salvation, according to thy word.

⁴²So shall I have wherewith to answer him that reproacheth me: for I trust in thy word.

⁴³And take not the word of truth utterly out of my mouth; for I have hoped in thy judgments.

[44]So shall I keep thy law continually for ever and ever.

[45]And I will walk at liberty: for I seek thy precepts.

[46]I will speak of thy testimonies also before kings, and will not be ashamed.

[47]And I will delight myself in thy commandments, which I have loved.

[48]My hands also will I lift up unto thy commandments, which I have loved; and I will meditate in thy statutes.

ZAIN

[49]Remember the word unto thy servant, upon which thou hast caused me to hope.

[50]This *is* my comfort in my affliction: for thy word hath quickened me.

[51]The proud have had me greatly in derision: *yet* have I not declined from thy law.

[52]I remembered thy judgments of old, O LORD; and have comforted myself.

[53]Horror hath taken hold upon me because of the wicked that forsake thy law.

[54]Thy statutes have been my songs in the house of my pilgrimage.

[55]I have remembered thy name, O LORD, in the night, and have kept thy law.

[56]This I had, because I kept thy precepts.

CHETH.

[57]*Thou art* my portion, O LORD: I have said that I would keep thy words.

[58]I intreated thy favour with *my* whole heart: be merciful unto me according to thy word.

[59]I thought on my ways, and turned my feet unto thy testimonies.

[60]I made haste, and delayed not to keep thy commandments.

[61]The bands of the wicked have robbed me: *but* I have not forgotten thy law.

[62]At midnight I will rise to give thanks unto thee because of thy righteous judgments.

[63]I *am* a companion of all *them* that fear thee, and of them that keep thy precepts.

[64]The earth, O LORD, is full of thy mercy: teach me thy statutes.

TETH.

[65]Thou hast dealt well with thy servant, O LORD, according unto thy word.

[66]Teach me good judgment and knowledge: for I have believed thy commandments.

[67]Before I was afflicted I went astray: but now have I kept thy word.

[68]Thou *art* good, and doest good; teach me thy statutes.

[69]The proud have forged a lie against me: *but* I will keep thy precepts with *my* whole heart.

⁷⁰Their heart is as fat as grease; *but* I delight in thy law.

⁷¹*It is* good for me that I have been afflicted; that I might learn thy statutes.

⁷²The law of thy mouth *is* better unto me than thousands of gold and silver.

JOD.

⁷³Thy hands have made me and fashioned me: give me understanding, that I may learn thy commandments.

⁷⁴They that fear thee will be glad when they see me; because I have hoped in thy word.

⁷⁵I know, O LORD, that thy judgments *are* right, and that *thou* in faithfulness hast afflicted me.

⁷⁶Let, I pray thee, thy merciful kindness be for my comfort, according to thy word unto thy servant.

⁷⁷Let thy tender mercies come unto me, that I may live: for thy law *is* my delight.

⁷⁸Let the proud be ashamed; for they dealt perversely with me without a cause: *but* I will meditate in thy precepts.

⁷⁹Let those that fear thee turn unto me, and those that have known thy testimonies.

⁸⁰Let my heart be sound in thy statutes; that I be not ashamed.

CAPH.

⁸¹My soul fainteth for thy salvation: *but* I hope in thy word.

⁸²Mine eyes fail for thy word, saying, When wilt thou comfort me?

⁸³For I am become like a bottle in the smoke; *yet* do I not forget thy statutes.

⁸⁴How many *are* the days of thy servant? when wilt thou execute judgment on them that persecute me?

⁸⁵The proud have digged pits for me, which *are* not after thy law.

⁸⁶All thy commandments *are* faithful: they persecute me wrongfully; help thou me.

⁸⁷They had almost consumed me upon earth; but I forsook not thy precepts.

⁸⁸Quicken me after thy lovingkindness; so shall I keep the testimony of thy mouth.

LAMED.

⁸⁹For ever, O LORD, thy word is settled in heaven.

⁹⁰Thy faithfulness *is* unto all generations: thou hast established the earth, and it abideth.

⁹¹They continue this day according to thine ordinances: for all *are* thy servants.

[92]Unless thy law *had been* my delights, I should then have perished in mine affliction.

[93]I will never forget thy precepts: for with them thou hast quickened me.

[94]I *am* thine, save me; for I have sought thy precepts.

[95]The wicked have waited for me to destroy me: *but* I will consider thy testimonies.

[96]I have seen an end of all perfection: *but* thy commandment *is* exceeding broad.

MEM.

[97]O how love I thy law! it *is* my meditation all the day.

[98]Thou through thy commandments hast made me wiser than mine enemies: for they *are* ever with me.

[99]I have more understanding than all my teachers: for thy testimonies *are* my meditation.

[100]I understand more than the ancients, because I keep thy precepts.

[101]I have refrained my feet from every evil way, that I might keep thy word.

[102]I have not departed from thy judgments: for thou hast taught me.

[103]How sweet are thy words unto my taste! *yea, sweeter* than honey to my mouth!

[104]Through thy precepts I get understanding: therefore I hate every false way.

NUN.

[105]Thy word *is* a lamp unto my feet, and a light unto my path.

[106]I have sworn, and I will perform *it,* that I will keep thy righteous judgments.

[107]I am afflicted very much: quicken me, O LORD, according unto thy word.

[108]Accept, I beseech thee, the freewill offerings of my mouth, O LORD, and teach me thy judgments.

[109]My soul *is* continually in my hand: yet do I not forget thy law.

[110]The wicked have laid a snare for me: yet I erred not from thy precepts.

[111]Thy testimonies have I taken as an heritage for ever: for they *are* the rejoicing of my heart.

[112]I have inclined mine heart to perform thy statutes alway, *even unto* the end.

SAMECH.

[113]I hate *vain* thoughts: but thy law do I love.

[114]Thou *art* my hiding place and my shield: I hope in thy word.

[115]Depart from me, ye evildoers: for I will keep the commandments of my God.

[116]Uphold me according unto thy word, that I may live: and let me not be ashamed of my hope.

[117]Hold thou me up, and I shall be safe: and I will have respect unto thy statutes continually.

[118]Thou hast trodden down all them that err from thy statutes: for their deceit *is* falsehood.

[119]Thou puttest away all the wicked of the earth *like* dross: therefore I love thy testimonies.

[120]My flesh trembleth for fear of thee; and I am afraid of thy judgments.

AIN.

[121]I have done judgment and justice: leave me not to mine oppressors.

[122]Be surety for thy servant for good: let not the proud oppress me.

[123]Mine eyes fail for thy salvation, and for the word of thy righteousness.

[124]Deal with thy servant according unto thy mercy, and teach me thy statutes.

[125]I *am* thy servant; give me understanding, that I may know thy testimonies.

[126]*It is* time for *thee,* LORD, to work: *for* they have made void thy law.

[127]Therefore I love thy commandments above gold; yea, above fine gold.

[128]Therefore I esteem all *thy* precepts *concerning* all *things to be* right; *and* I hate every false way.

PE.

[129]Thy testimonies *are* wonderful: therefore doth my soul keep them.

[130]The entrance of thy words giveth light; it giveth understanding unto the simple.

[131]I opened my mouth, and panted: for I longed for thy commandments.

[132]Look thou upon me, and be merciful unto me, as thou usest to do unto those that love thy name.

[133]Order my steps in thy word: and let not any iniquity have dominion over me.

[134]Deliver me from the oppression of man: so will I keep thy precepts.

[135]Make thy face to shine upon thy servant; and teach me thy statutes.

[136]Rivers of waters run down mine eyes, because they keep not thy law.

TZADDE.

[137]Righteous *art* thou, O LORD, and upright *are* thy judgments.

[138]Thy testimonies *that* thou hast commanded *are* righteous and very faithful.

[139]My zeal hath consumed me, because mine enemies have forgotten thy words.

¹⁴⁰Thy word *is* very pure: therefore thy servant loveth it.

¹⁴¹I *am* small and despised: *yet* do not I forget thy precepts.

¹⁴²Thy righteousness *is* an everlasting righteousness, and thy law *is* the truth.

¹⁴³Trouble and anguish have taken hold on me: *yet* thy commandments *are* my delights.

¹⁴⁴The righteousness of thy testimonies *is* everlasting: give me understanding, and I shall live.

KOPH.

¹⁴⁵I cried with *my* whole heart; hear me, O LORD: I will keep thy statutes.

¹⁴⁶I cried unto thee; save me, and I shall keep thy testimonies.

¹⁴⁷I prevented the dawning of the morning, and cried: I hoped in thy word.

¹⁴⁸Mine eyes prevent the *night* watches, that I might meditate in thy word.

¹⁴⁹Hear my voice according unto thy lovingkindness: O LORD, quicken me according to thy judgment.

¹⁵⁰They draw nigh that follow after mischief: they are far from thy law.

¹⁵¹Thou *art* near, O LORD; and all thy commandments *are* truth.

¹⁵²Concerning thy testimonies, I have known of old that thou hast founded them for ever.

RESH.

¹⁵³Consider mine affliction, and deliver me: for I do not forget thy law.

¹⁵⁴Plead my cause, and deliver me: quicken me according to thy word.

¹⁵⁵Salvation *is* far from the wicked: for they seek not thy statutes.

¹⁵⁶Great *are* thy tender mercies, O LORD: quicken me according to thy judgments.

¹⁵⁷Many *are* my persecutors and mine enemies; *yet* do I not decline from thy testimonies.

¹⁵⁸I beheld the transgressors, and was grieved; because they kept not thy word.

¹⁵⁹Consider how I love thy precepts: quicken me, O LORD, according to thy lovingkindness.

¹⁶⁰Thy word *is* true *from* the beginning: and every one of thy righteous judgments *endureth* for ever.

SCHIN.

¹⁶¹Princes have persecuted me without a cause: but my heart standeth in awe of thy word.

¹⁶²I rejoice at thy word, as one that findeth great spoil.

¹⁶³I hate and abhor lying: *but* thy law do I love.

¹⁶⁴Seven times a day do I praise thee because of thy righteous judgments.

¹⁶⁵Great peace have they which love thy law: and nothing shall offend them.

¹⁶⁶LORD, I have hoped for thy salvation, and done thy commandments.

¹⁶⁷My soul hath kept thy testimonies; and I love them exceedingly.

¹⁶⁸I have kept thy precepts and thy testimonies: for all my ways *are* before thee.

TAU.

¹⁶⁹Let my cry come near before thee, O LORD: give me understanding according to thy word.

¹⁷⁰Let my supplication come before thee: deliver me according to thy word.

¹⁷¹My lips shall utter praise, when thou hast taught me thy statutes.

¹⁷²My tongue shall speak of thy word: for all thy commandments *are* righteousness.

¹⁷³Let thine hand help me; for I have chosen thy precepts.

¹⁷⁴I have longed for thy salvation, O LORD; and thy law *is* my delight.

¹⁷⁵Let my soul live, and it shall praise thee; and let thy judgments help me.

¹⁷⁶I have gone astray like a lost sheep; seek thy servant; for I do not forget thy commandments.

Psalm 120

A Song of degrees.

¹In my distress I cried unto the LORD, and he heard me.

²Deliver my soul, O LORD, from lying lips, *and* from a deceitful tongue.

³What shall be given unto thee? or what shall be done unto thee, thou false tongue?

⁴Sharp arrows of the mighty, with coals of juniper.

⁵Woe is me, that I sojourn in Mesech, *that* I dwell in the tents of Kedar!

⁶My soul hath long dwelt with him that hateth peace.

⁷I *am for* peace: but when I speak, they *are* for war.

Psalm 121

A Song of degrees.

[1]I will lift up mine eyes unto the hills, from whence cometh my help.
[2]My help *cometh* from the LORD, which made heaven and earth.
[3]He will not suffer thy foot to be moved: he that keepeth thee will not slumber.
[4]Behold, he that keepeth Israel shall neither slumber nor sleep.
[5]The LORD *is* thy keeper: the LORD *is* thy shade upon thy right hand.
[6]The sun shall not smite thee by day, nor the moon by night.
[7]The LORD shall preserve thee from all evil: he shall preserve thy soul.
[8]The LORD shall preserve thy going out and thy coming in from this time forth, and even for evermore.

Psalm 122

A Song of degrees of David.

[1]I was glad when they said unto me, Let us go into the house of the LORD.
[2]Our feet shall stand within thy gates, O Jerusalem.
[3]Jerusalem is builded as a city that is compact together:
[4]Whither the tribes go up, the tribes of the LORD, unto the testimony of Israel, to give thanks unto the name of the LORD.
[5]For there are set thrones of judgment, the thrones of the house of David.
[6]Pray for the peace of Jerusalem: they shall prosper that love thee.
[7]Peace be within thy walls, *and* prosperity within thy palaces.
[8]For my brethren and companions' sakes, I will now say, Peace *be* within thee.
[9]Because of the house of the LORD our God I will seek thy good.

Psalm 123

A Song of degrees.

[1]Unto thee lift I up mine eyes, O thou that dwellest in the heavens.
[2]Behold, as the eyes of servants *look* unto the hand of their masters, *and* as the eyes of a
  maiden unto the hand of her mistress; so our eyes *wait* upon the LORD our God,
  until that he have mercy upon us.
[3]Have mercy upon us, O LORD, have mercy upon us: for we are exceedingly filled with
  contempt.
[4]Our soul is exceedingly filled with the scorning of those that are at ease, *and* with the
  contempt of the proud.

Psalm 124

A Song of degrees of David.

[1]If *it had not been* the LORD who was on our side, now may Israel say;
[2]If *it had not been* the LORD who was on our side, when men rose up against us:
[3]Then they had swallowed us up quick, when their wrath was kindled against us:
[4]Then the waters had overwhelmed us, the stream had gone over our soul:
[5]Then the proud waters had gone over our soul.
[6]Blessed *be* the LORD, who hath not given us *as* a prey to their teeth.
[7]Our soul is escaped as a bird out of the snare of the fowlers: the snare is broken, and we are
  escaped.
[8]Our help *is* in the name of the LORD, who made heaven and earth.

Psalm 125

A Song of degrees.

[1]They that trust in the LORD *shall be* as mount Zion, *which* cannot be removed, *but*
abideth for ever.
[2]As the mountains *are* round about Jerusalem, so the LORD *is* round about his people from
  henceforth even for ever.

³For the rod of the wicked shall not rest upon the lot of the righteous; lest the righteous put forth their hands unto iniquity.

⁴Do good, O LORD, unto *those that be* good, and *to them that are* upright in their hearts.

⁵As for such as turn aside unto their crooked ways, the LORD shall lead them forth with the workers of iniquity: *but* peace *shall be* upon Israel.

Psalm 126

A Song of degrees.

¹When the LORD turned again the captivity of Zion, we were like them that dream.

²Then was our mouth filled with laughter, and our tongue with singing: then said they among the heathen, The LORD hath done great things for them.

³The LORD hath done great things for us; *whereof* we are glad.

⁴Turn again our captivity, O LORD, as the streams in the south.

⁵They that sow in tears shall reap in joy.

⁶He that goeth forth and weepeth, bearing precious seed, shall doubtless come again with rejoicing, bringing his sheaves *with him.*

Psalm 127

A Song of degrees for Solomon.

¹Except the LORD build the house, they labour in vain that build it: except the LORD keep the city, the watchman waketh *but* in vain.

²*It is* vain for you to rise up early, to sit up late, to eat the bread of sorrows: *for* so he giveth his beloved sleep.

³Lo, children *are* an heritage of the LORD: *and* the fruit of the womb *is his* reward.

⁴As arrows *are* in the hand of a mighty man; so *are* children of the youth.

⁵Happy *is* the man that hath his quiver full of them: they shall not be ashamed, but they shall speak with the enemies in the gate.

Psalm 128

A Song of degrees.

[1]Blessed *is* every one that feareth the LORD; that walketh in his ways.
[2]For thou shalt eat the labour of thine hands: happy *shalt* thou *be,* and *it shall be* well with
  thee.
[3]Thy wife *shall be* as a fruitful vine by the sides of thine house: thy children like olive plants
  round about thy table.
[4]Behold, that thus shall the man be blessed that feareth the LORD.
[5]The LORD shall bless thee out of Zion: and thou shalt see the good of Jerusalem all the days
  of thy life.
[6]Yea, thou shalt see thy children's children, *and* peace upon Israel.

Psalm 129

A Song of degrees.

[1]Many a time have they afflicted me from my youth, may Israel now say:
[2]Many a time have they afflicted me from my youth: yet they have not prevailed against me.
[3]The plowers plowed upon my back: they made long their furrows.
[4]The LORD *is* righteous: he hath cut asunder the cords of the wicked.
[5]Let them all be confounded and turned back that hate Zion.
[6]Let them be as the grass *upon* the housetops, which withereth afore it groweth up:
[7]Wherewith the mower filleth not his hand; nor he that bindeth sheaves his bosom.
[8]Neither do they which go by say, The blessing of the LORD *be* upon you: we bless you in
  the name of the LORD.

Psalm 130

A Song of degrees.

¹Out of the depths have I cried unto thee, O LORD.

²Lord, hear my voice: let thine ears be attentive to the voice of my supplications.

³If thou, LORD, shouldest mark iniquities, O Lord, who shall stand?

⁴But *there is* forgiveness with thee, that thou mayest be feared.

⁵I wait for the LORD, my soul doth wait, and in his word do I hope.

⁶My soul *waiteth* for the Lord more than they that watch for the morning: *I say, more than* they that watch for the morning.

⁷Let Israel hope in the LORD: for with the LORD *there is* mercy, and with him *is* plenteous redemption.

⁸And he shall redeem Israel from all his iniquities.

Psalm 131

A Song of degrees of David.

¹LORD, my heart is not haughty, nor mine eyes lofty: neither do I exercise myself in great matters, or in things too high for me.

²Surely I have behaved and quieted myself, as a child that is weaned of his mother: my soul *is* even as a weaned child.

³Let Israel hope in the LORD from henceforth and for ever.

Psalm 132

A Song of degrees.

¹LORD, remember David, *and* all his afflictions:

²How he sware unto the LORD, *and* vowed unto the mighty *God* of Jacob;

³Surely I will not come into the tabernacle of my house, nor go up into my bed;

⁴I will not give sleep to mine eyes, *or* slumber to mine eyelids,

⁵Until I find out a place for the LORD, an habitation for the mighty *God* of Jacob.

⁶Lo, we heard of it at Ephratah: we found it in the fields of the wood.

⁷We will go into his tabernacles: we will worship at his footstool.

⁸Arise, O LORD, into thy rest; thou, and the ark of thy strength.

^{9}Let thy priests be clothed with righteousness; and let thy saints shout for joy.

^{10}For thy servant David's sake turn not away the face of thine anointed.

^{11}The LORD hath sworn *in* truth unto David; he will not turn from it; Of the fruit of thy body will I set upon thy throne.

^{12}If thy children will keep my covenant and my testimony that I shall teach them, their children shall also sit upon thy throne for evermore.

^{13}For the LORD hath chosen Zion; he hath desired *it* for his habitation.

^{14}This *is* my rest for ever: here will I dwell; for I have desired it.

^{15}I will abundantly bless her provision: I will satisfy her poor with bread.

^{16}I will also clothe her priests with salvation: and her saints shall shout aloud for joy.

^{17}There will I make the horn of David to bud: I have ordained a lamp for mine anointed.

^{18}His enemies will I clothe with shame: but upon himself shall his crown flourish.

Psalm 133

A Song of degrees of David.

^{1}Behold, how good and how pleasant *it is* for brethren to dwell together in unity!

^{2}*It is* like the precious ointment upon the head, that ran down upon the beard, *even* Aaron's beard: that went down to the skirts of his garments;

^{3}As the dew of Hermon, *and as the dew* that descended upon the mountains of Zion: for there the LORD commanded the blessing, *even* life for evermore.

Psalm 134

A Song of degrees.

^{1}Behold, bless ye the LORD, all *ye* servants of the LORD, which by night stand in the house of the LORD.

^{2}Lift up your hands *in* the sanctuary, and bless the LORD.

^{3}The LORD that made heaven and earth bless thee out of Zion.

Psalm 135

^{1}Praise ye the LORD. Praise ye the name of the LORD; praise *him,* O ye servants of the LORD.

^{2}Ye that stand in the house of the LORD, in the courts of the house of our God,

^{3}Praise the LORD; for the LORD *is* good: sing praises unto his name; for *it is* pleasant.

^{4}For the LORD hath chosen Jacob unto himself, *and* Israel for his peculiar treasure.

^{5}For I know that the LORD *is* great, and *that* our Lord *is* above all gods.

^{6}Whatsoever the LORD pleased, *that* did he in heaven, and in earth, in the seas, and all deep places.

^{7}He causeth the vapours to ascend from the ends of the earth; he maketh lightnings for the rain; he bringeth the wind out of his treasuries.

^{8}Who smote the firstborn of Egypt, both of man and beast.

^{9}*Who* sent tokens and wonders into the midst of thee, O Egypt, upon Pharaoh, and upon all his servants.

^{10}Who smote great nations, and slew mighty kings;

^{11}Sihon king of the Amorites, and Og king of Bashan, and all the kingdoms of Canaan:

^{12}And gave their land *for* an heritage, an heritage unto Israel his people.

^{13}Thy name, O LORD, *endureth* for ever; *and* thy memorial, O LORD, throughout all generations.

^{14}For the LORD will judge his people, and he will repent himself concerning his servants.

^{15}The idols of the heathen *are* silver and gold, the work of men's hands.

^{16}They have mouths, but they speak not; eyes have they, but they see not;

^{17}They have ears, but they hear not; neither is there *any* breath in their mouths.

^{18}They that make them are like unto them: *so is* every one that trusteth in them.

^{19}Bless the LORD, O house of Israel: bless the LORD, O house of Aaron:

^{20}Bless the LORD, O house of Levi: ye that fear the LORD, bless the LORD.

^{21}Blessed be the LORD out of Zion, which dwelleth at Jerusalem. Praise ye the LORD.

Psalm 136

^{1}O give thanks unto the LORD; for *he is* good: for his mercy *endureth* for ever.

^{2}O give thanks unto the God of gods: for his mercy *endureth* for ever.

^{3}O give thanks to the Lord of lords: for his mercy *endureth* for ever.

^{4}To him who alone doeth great wonders: for his mercy *endureth* for ever.

^{5}To him that by wisdom made the heavens: for his mercy *endureth* for ever.

^{6}To him that stretched out the earth above the waters: for his mercy *endureth* for ever.

^{7}To him that made great lights: for his mercy *endureth* for ever:

^{8}The sun to rule by day: for his mercy *endureth* for ever:

⁹The moon and stars to rule by night: for his mercy *endureth* for ever.

¹⁰To him that smote Egypt in their firstborn: for his mercy *endureth* for ever:

¹¹And brought out Israel from among them: for his mercy *endureth* for ever:

¹²With a strong hand, and with a stretched out arm: for his mercy *endureth* for ever.

¹³To him which divided the Red sea into parts: for his mercy *endureth* for ever:

¹⁴And made Israel to pass through the midst of it: for his mercy *endureth* for ever:

¹⁵But overthrew Pharaoh and his host in the Red sea: for his mercy *endureth* for ever.

¹⁶To him which led his people through the wilderness: for his mercy *endureth* for ever.

¹⁷To him which smote great kings: for his mercy *endureth* for ever:

¹⁸And slew famous kings: for his mercy *endureth* for ever:

¹⁹Sihon king of the Amorites: for his mercy *endureth* for ever:

²⁰And Og the king of Bashan: for his mercy *endureth* for ever:

²¹And gave their land for an heritage: for his mercy *endureth* for ever:

²²*Even* an heritage unto Israel his servant: for his mercy *endureth* for ever.

²³Who remembered us in our low estate: for his mercy *endureth* for ever:

²⁴And hath redeemed us from our enemies: for his mercy *endureth* for ever.

²⁵Who giveth food to all flesh: for his mercy *endureth* for ever.

²⁶O give thanks unto the God of heaven: for his mercy *endureth* for ever.

Psalm 137

¹By the rivers of Babylon, there we sat down, yea, we wept, when we remembered Zion.

²We hanged our harps upon the willows in the midst thereof.

³For there they that carried us away captive required of us a song; and they that wasted us *required of us* mirth, *saying,* Sing us *one* of the songs of Zion.

⁴How shall we sing the LORD'S song in a strange land?

⁵If I forget thee, O Jerusalem, let my right hand forget *her cunning.*

⁶If I do not remember thee, let my tongue cleave to the roof of my mouth; if I prefer not Jerusalem above my chief joy.

⁷Remember, O LORD, the children of Edom in the day of Jerusalem; who said, Rase *it,* rase *it, even* to the foundation thereof.

⁸O daughter of Babylon, who art to be destroyed; happy *shall he be,* that rewardeth thee as thou hast served us.

⁹Happy *shall he be,* that taketh and dasheth thy little ones against the stones.

Psalm 138

A *Psalm* of David.

[1]I will praise thee with my whole heart: before the gods will I sing praise unto thee.
[2]I will worship toward thy holy temple, and praise thy name for thy lovingkindness and for thy truth: for thou hast magnified thy word above all thy name.
[3]In the day when I cried thou answeredst me, *and* strengthenedst me *with* strength in my soul.
[4]All the kings of the earth shall praise thee, O LORD, when they hear the words of thy mouth.
[5]Yea, they shall sing in the ways of the LORD: for great *is* the glory of the LORD.
[6]Though the LORD *be* high, yet hath he respect unto the lowly: but the proud he knoweth afar off.
[7]Though I walk in the midst of trouble, thou wilt revive me: thou shalt stretch forth thine hand against the wrath of mine enemies, and thy right hand shall save me.
[8]The LORD will perfect *that which* concerneth me: thy mercy, O LORD, *endureth* for ever: forsake not the works of thine own hands.

Psalm 139

To the chief Musician, A Psalm of David.

[1]O LORD, thou hast searched me, and known *me.*
[2]Thou knowest my downsitting and mine uprising, thou understandest my thought afar off.
[3]Thou compassest my path and my lying down, and art acquainted *with* all my ways.
[4]For *there is* not a word in my tongue, *but,* lo, O LORD, thou knowest it altogether.
[5]Thou hast beset me behind and before, and laid thine hand upon me.
[6]*Such* knowledge *is* too wonderful for me; it is high, I cannot *attain* unto it.
[7]Whither shall I go from thy spirit? or whither shall I flee from thy presence?
[8]If I ascend up into heaven, thou *art* there: if I make my bed in hell, behold, thou *art there.*
[9]*If* I take the wings of the morning, *and* dwell in the uttermost parts of the sea;
[10]Even there shall thy hand lead me, and thy right hand shall hold me.
[11]If I say, Surely the darkness shall cover me; even the night shall be light about me.
[12]Yea, the darkness hideth not from thee; but the night shineth as the day: the darkness and the light *are* both alike *to thee.*

¹³For thou hast possessed my reins: thou hast covered me in my mother's womb.

¹⁴I will praise thee; for I am fearfully *and* wonderfully made: marvellous *are* thy works; and *that* my soul knoweth right well.

¹⁵My substance was not hid from thee, when I was made in secret, *and* curiously wrought in the lowest parts of the earth.

¹⁶Thine eyes did see my substance, yet being unperfect; and in thy book all *my members* were written, *which* in continuance were fashioned, when *as yet there was* none of them.

¹⁷How precious also are thy thoughts unto me, O God! how great is the sum of them!

¹⁸*If* I should count them, they are more in number than the sand: when I awake, I am still with thee.

¹⁹Surely thou wilt slay the wicked, O God: depart from me therefore, ye bloody men.

²⁰For they speak against thee wickedly, *and* thine enemies take *thy name* in vain.

²¹Do not I hate them, O LORD, that hate thee? and am not I grieved with those that rise up against thee?

²²I hate them with perfect hatred: I count them mine enemies.

²³Search me, O God, and know my heart: try me, and know my thoughts:

²⁴And see if *there be any* wicked way in me, and lead me in the way everlasting.

Psalm 140

To the chief Musician, A Psalm of David.

¹Deliver me, O LORD, from the evil man: preserve me from the violent man;

²Which imagine mischiefs in *their* heart; continually are they gathered together *for* war.

³They have sharpened their tongues like a serpent; adders' poison *is* under their lips. Selah.

⁴Keep me, O LORD, from the hands of the wicked; preserve me from the violent man; who have purposed to overthrow my goings.

⁵The proud have hid a snare for me, and cords; they have spread a net by the wayside; they have set gins for me. Selah.

⁶I said unto the LORD, Thou *art* my God: hear the voice of my supplications, O LORD.

⁷O GOD the Lord, the strength of my salvation, thou hast covered my head in the day of battle.

⁸Grant not, O LORD, the desires of the wicked: further not his wicked device; *lest* they exalt themselves. Selah.

⁹*As for* the head of those that compass me about, let the mischief of their own lips cover them.

¹⁰Let burning coals fall upon them: let them be cast into the fire; into deep pits, that they rise not up again.
¹¹Let not an evil speaker be established in the earth: evil shall hunt the violent man to overthrow *him.*
¹²I know that the LORD will maintain the cause of the afflicted, *and* the right of the poor.
¹³Surely the righteous shall give thanks unto thy name: the upright shall dwell in thy presence.

Psalm 141

A Psalm of David.

¹LORD, I cry unto thee: make haste unto me; give ear unto my voice, when I cry unto thee.
²Let my prayer be set forth before thee *as* incense; *and* the lifting up of my hands *as* the evening sacrifice.
³Set a watch, O LORD, before my mouth; keep the door of my lips.
⁴Incline not my heart to *any* evil thing, to practise wicked works with men that work iniquity: and let me not eat of their dainties.
⁵Let the righteous smite me; *it shall be* a kindness: and let him reprove me; *it shall be* an excellent oil, *which* shall not break my head: for yet my prayer also *shall be* in their calamities.
⁶When their judges are overthrown in stony places, they shall hear my words; for they are sweet.
⁷Our bones are scattered at the grave's mouth, as when one cutteth and cleaveth *wood* upon the earth.
⁸But mine eyes *are* unto thee, O GOD the Lord: in thee is my trust; leave not my soul destitute.
⁹Keep me from the snares *which* they have laid for me, and the gins of the workers of iniquity.
¹⁰Let the wicked fall into their own nets, whilst that I withal escape.

Psalm 142

Maschil of David; A Prayer when he was in the cave.

¹I cried unto the LORD with my voice; with my voice unto the LORD did I make my supplication.

²I poured out my complaint before him; I shewed before him my trouble.

³When my spirit was overwhelmed within me, then thou knewest my path. In the way wherein I walked have they privily laid a snare for me.

⁴I looked on *my* right hand, and beheld, but *there was* no man that would know me: refuge failed me; no man cared for my soul.

⁵I cried unto thee, O LORD: I said, Thou *art* my refuge *and* my portion in the land of the living.

⁶Attend unto my cry; for I am brought very low: deliver me from my persecutors; for they are stronger than I.

⁷Bring my soul out of prison, that I may praise thy name: the righteous shall compass me about; for thou shalt deal bountifully with me.

Psalm 143

A Psalm of David.

¹Hear my prayer, O LORD, give ear to my supplications: in thy faithfulness answer me, *and* in thy righteousness.

²And enter not into judgment with thy servant: for in thy sight shall no man living be justified.

³For the enemy hath persecuted my soul; he hath smitten my life down to the ground; he hath made me to dwell in darkness, as those that have been long dead.

⁴Therefore is my spirit overwhelmed within me; my heart within me is desolate.

⁵I remember the days of old; I meditate on all thy works; I muse on the work of thy hands.

⁶I stretch forth my hands unto thee: my soul *thirsteth* after thee, as a thirsty land. Selah.

⁷Hear me speedily, O LORD: my spirit faileth: hide not thy face from me, lest I be like unto them that go down into the pit.

⁸Cause me to hear thy lovingkindness in the morning; for in thee do I trust: cause me to know the way wherein I should walk; for I lift up my soul unto thee.

⁹Deliver me, O LORD, from mine enemies: I flee unto thee to hide me.

¹⁰Teach me to do thy will; for thou *art* my God: thy spirit *is* good; lead me into the land of uprightness.

[11]Quicken me, O LORD, for thy name's sake: for thy righteousness' sake bring my soul out of trouble.

[12]And of thy mercy cut off mine enemies, and destroy all them that afflict my soul: for I *am* thy servant.

Psalm 144

A *Psalm* of David.

[1]Blessed *be* the LORD my strength, which teacheth my hands to war, *and* my fingers to fight:

[2]My goodness, and my fortress; my high tower, and my deliverer; my shield, and *he* in whom I trust; who subdueth my people under me.

[3]LORD, what *is* man, that thou takest knowledge of him! *or* the son of man, that thou makest account of him!

[4]Man is like to vanity: his days *are* as a shadow that passeth away.

[5]Bow thy heavens, O LORD, and come down: touch the mountains, and they shall smoke.

[6]Cast forth lightning, and scatter them: shoot out thine arrows, and destroy them.

[7]Send thine hand from above; rid me, and deliver me out of great waters, from the hand of strange children;

[8]Whose mouth speaketh vanity, and their right hand *is* a right hand of falsehood.

[9]I will sing a new song unto thee, O God: upon a psaltery *and* an instrument of ten strings will I sing praises unto thee.

[10]*It is he* that giveth salvation unto kings: who delivereth David his servant from the hurtful sword.

[11]Rid me, and deliver me from the hand of strange children, whose mouth speaketh vanity, and their right hand *is* a right hand of falsehood:

[12]That our sons *may be* as plants grown up in their youth; *that* our daughters *may be* as corner stones, polished *after* the similitude of a palace:

[13]*That* our garners *may be* full, affording all manner of store: *that* our sheep may bring forth thousands and ten thousands in our streets:

[14]*That* our oxen *may be* strong to labour; *that there be* no breaking in, nor going out; that *there be* no complaining in our streets.

[15]Happy *is that* people, that is in such a case: *yea,* happy *is that* people, whose God *is* the LORD.

Psalm 145

David's *Psalm* of praise.

[1]I will extol thee, my God, O king; and I will bless thy name for ever and ever.

[2]Every day will I bless thee; and I will praise thy name for ever and ever.

[3]Great *is* the LORD, and greatly to be praised; and his greatness *is* unsearchable.

[4]One generation shall praise thy works to another, and shall declare thy mighty acts.

[5]I will speak of the glorious honour of thy majesty, and of thy wondrous works.

[6]And *men* shall speak of the might of thy terrible acts: and I will declare thy greatness.

[7]They shall abundantly utter the memory of thy great goodness, and shall sing of thy righteousness.

[8]The LORD *is* gracious, and full of compassion; slow to anger, and of great mercy.

[9]The LORD *is* good to all: and his tender mercies *are* over all his works.

[10]All thy works shall praise thee, O LORD; and thy saints shall bless thee.

[11]They shall speak of the glory of thy kingdom, and talk of thy power;

[12]To make known to the sons of men his mighty acts, and the glorious majesty of his kingdom.

[13]Thy kingdom *is* an everlasting kingdom, and thy dominion *endureth* throughout all generations.

[14]The LORD upholdeth all that fall, and raiseth up all *those that be* bowed down.

[15]The eyes of all wait upon thee; and thou givest them their meat in due season.

[16]Thou openest thine hand, and satisfiest the desire of every living thing.

[17]The LORD *is* righteous in all his ways, and holy in all his works.

[18]The LORD *is* nigh unto all them that call upon him, to all that call upon him in truth.

[19]He will fulfil the desire of them that fear him: he also will hear their cry, and will save them.

[20]The LORD preserveth all them that love him: but all the wicked will he destroy.

[21]My mouth shall speak the praise of the LORD: and let all flesh bless his holy name for ever and ever.

Psalm 146

[1]Praise ye the LORD. Praise the LORD, O my soul.

[2]While I live will I praise the LORD: I will sing praises unto my God while I have any being.

[3]Put not your trust in princes, *nor* in the son of man, in whom *there is* no help.

[4]His breath goeth forth, he returneth to his earth; in that very day his thoughts perish.

[5]Happy *is he* that *hath* the God of Jacob for his help, whose hope *is* in the LORD his God:

⁶Which made heaven, and earth, the sea, and all that therein *is:* which keepeth truth for ever:
⁷Which executeth judgment for the oppressed: which giveth food to the hungry. The LORD looseth the prisoners:
⁸The LORD openeth *the eyes of* the blind: the LORD raiseth them that are bowed down: the LORD loveth the righteous:
⁹The LORD preserveth the strangers; he relieveth the fatherless and widow: but the way of the wicked he turneth upside down.
¹⁰The LORD shall reign for ever, *even* thy God, O Zion, unto all generations. Praise ye the LORD.

Psalm 147

¹Praise ye the LORD: for *it is* good to sing praises unto our God; for *it is* pleasant; *and* praise is comely.
²The LORD doth build up Jerusalem: he gathereth together the outcasts of Israel.
³He healeth the broken in heart, and bindeth up their wounds.
⁴He telleth the number of the stars; he calleth them all by *their* names.
⁵Great *is* our Lord, and of great power: his understanding *is* infinite.
⁶The LORD lifteth up the meek: he casteth the wicked down to the ground.
⁷Sing unto the LORD with thanksgiving; sing praise upon the harp unto our God:
⁸Who covereth the heaven with clouds, who prepareth rain for the earth, who maketh grass to grow upon the mountains.
⁹He giveth to the beast his food, *and* to the young ravens which cry.
¹⁰He delighteth not in the strength of the horse: he taketh not pleasure in the legs of a man.
¹¹The LORD taketh pleasure in them that fear him, in those that hope in his mercy.
¹²Praise the LORD, O Jerusalem; praise thy God, O Zion.
¹³For he hath strengthened the bars of thy gates; he hath blessed thy children within thee.
¹⁴He maketh peace *in* thy borders, *and* filleth thee with the finest of the wheat.
¹⁵He sendeth forth his commandment *upon* earth: his word runneth very swiftly.
¹⁶He giveth snow like wool: he scattereth the hoar frost like ashes.
¹⁷He casteth forth his ice like morsels: who can stand before his cold?
¹⁸He sendeth out his word, and melteth them: he causeth his wind to blow, *and* the waters flow.
¹⁹He sheweth his word unto Jacob, his statutes and his judgments unto Israel.
²⁰He hath not dealt so with any nation: and *as for his* judgments, they have not known them. Praise ye the LORD.

Psalm 148

¹Praise ye the LORD. Praise ye the LORD from the heavens: praise him in the heights.
²Praise ye him, all his angels: praise ye him, all his hosts.
³Praise ye him, sun and moon: praise him, all ye stars of light.
⁴Praise him, ye heavens of heavens, and ye waters that *be* above the heavens.
⁵Let them praise the name of the LORD: for he commanded, and they were created.
⁶He hath also stablished them for ever and ever: he hath made a decree which shall not pass.
⁷Praise the LORD from the earth, ye dragons, and all deeps:
⁸Fire, and hail; snow, and vapours; stormy wind fulfilling his word:
⁹Mountains, and all hills; fruitful trees, and all cedars:
¹⁰Beasts, and all cattle; creeping things, and flying fowl:
¹¹Kings of the earth, and all people; princes, and all judges of the earth:
¹²Both young men, and maidens; old men, and children:
¹³Let them praise the name of the LORD: for his name alone is excellent; his glory *is* above the earth and heaven.
¹⁴He also exalteth the horn of his people, the praise of all his saints; *even* of the children of Israel, a people near unto him. Praise ye the LORD.

Psalm 149

¹Praise ye the LORD. Sing unto the LORD a new song, *and* his praise in the congregation of saints.
²Let Israel rejoice in him that made him: let the children of Zion be joyful in their King.
³Let them praise his name in the dance: let them sing praises unto him with the timbrel and harp.
⁴For the LORD taketh pleasure in his people: he will beautify the meek with salvation.
⁵Let the saints be joyful in glory: let them sing aloud upon their beds.
⁶*Let* the high *praises* of God *be* in their mouth, and a twoedged sword in their hand;
⁷To execute vengeance upon the heathen, *and* punishments upon the people;
⁸To bind their kings with chains, and their nobles with fetters of iron;
⁹To execute upon them the judgment written: this honour have all his saints. Praise ye the LORD.

Psalm 150

¹Praise ye the LORD. Praise God in his sanctuary: praise him in the firmament of his power.

²Praise him for his mighty acts: praise him according to his excellent greatness.
³Praise him with the sound of the trumpet: praise him with the psaltery and harp.
⁴Praise him with the timbrel and dance: praise him with stringed instruments and organs.
⁵Praise him upon the loud cymbals: praise him upon the high sounding cymbals.
⁶Let every thing that hath breath praise the LORD. Praise ye the LORD.

The Proverbs

1 The proverbs of Solomon the son of David, king of Israel; [2]To know wisdom and instruction; to perceive the words of understanding; [3]To receive the instruction of wisdom, justice, and judgment, and equity; [4]To give subtilty to the simple, to the young man knowledge and discretion. [5]A wise *man* will hear, and will increase learning; and a man of understanding shall attain unto wise counsels: [6]To understand a proverb, and the interpretation; the words of the wise, and their dark sayings.

[7]The fear of the LORD *is* the beginning of knowledge: *but* fools despise wisdom and instruction. [8]My son, hear the instruction of thy father, and forsake not the law of thy mother: [9]For they *shall be* an ornament of grace unto thy head, and chains about thy neck.

[10]My son, if sinners entice thee, consent thou not. [11]If they say, Come with us, let us lay wait for blood, let us lurk privily for the innocent without cause: [12]Let us swallow them up alive as the grave; and whole, as those that go down into the pit: [13]We shall find all precious substance, we shall fill our houses with spoil: [14]Cast in thy lot among us; let us all have one purse: [15]My son, walk not thou in the way with them; refrain thy foot from their path: [16]For their feet run to evil, and make haste to shed blood. [17]Surely in vain the net is spread in the sight of any bird. [18]And they lay wait for their *own* blood; they lurk privily for their *own* lives. [19]So *are* the ways of every one that is greedy of gain; *which* taketh away the life of the owners thereof.

[20]Wisdom crieth without; she uttereth her voice in the streets: [21]She crieth in the chief place of concourse, in the openings of the gates: in the city she uttereth her words, *saying,* [22]How long, ye simple ones, will ye love simplicity? and the scorners delight in their scorning, and fools hate knowledge? [23]Turn you at my reproof: behold, I will pour out my spirit unto you, I will make known my words unto you.

[24]Because I have called, and ye refused; I have stretched out my hand, and no man regarded; [25]But ye have set at nought all my counsel, and would none of my reproof: [26]I also will laugh at your calamity; I will mock when your fear cometh; [27]When your fear cometh as desolation, and your destruction cometh as a whirlwind; when distress and anguish cometh upon you. [28]Then shall they call upon me, but I will not answer; they shall seek me early, but they shall not find me: [29]For that they hated knowledge, and did not choose the fear of the LORD: [30]They would none of my counsel: they despised all my reproof. [31]Therefore shall they eat of the fruit of their own way, and be filled with their own devices. [32]For the turning away of the simple shall slay them, and the prosperity of fools shall destroy them. [33]But whoso hearkeneth unto me shall dwell safely, and shall be quiet from fear of evil.

2 My son, if thou wilt receive my words, and hide my commandments with thee; [2]So that thou incline thine ear unto wisdom, *and* apply thine heart to understanding; [3]Yea, if thou criest after knowledge, *and* liftest up thy voice for understanding; [4]If thou seekest her as silver, and searchest for her as *for* hid treasures; [5]Then shalt thou understand the fear of the LORD, and find the knowledge of God. [6]For the LORD giveth wisdom: out of his mouth *cometh* knowledge and understanding. [7]He layeth up sound wisdom for the righteous: *he is* a buckler to them that walk uprightly. [8]He keepeth the paths of judgment, and preserveth the way of his saints. [9]Then shalt thou understand righteousness, and judgment, and equity; *yea,* every good path.

[10]When wisdom entereth into thine heart, and knowledge is pleasant unto thy soul; [11]Discretion shall preserve thee, understanding shall keep thee: [12]To deliver thee from the way of the evil *man,* from the man that speaketh froward things; [13]Who leave the paths of uprightness, to walk in the ways of darkness; [14]Who rejoice to do evil, *and* delight in the frowardness of the wicked; [15]Whose ways *are* crooked, and *they* froward in their paths: [16]To deliver thee from the strange woman, *even* from the stranger *which* flattereth with her words; [17]Which forsaketh the guide of her youth, and forgetteth the covenant of her God. [18]For her house inclineth unto death, and her paths unto the dead. [19]None that go unto her return again, neither take they hold of the paths of life. [20]That thou mayest walk in the way of good *men,* and keep the paths of the righteous. [21]For the upright shall dwell in the land, and the perfect shall remain in it. [22]But the wicked shall be cut off from the earth, and the transgressors shall be rooted out of it.

3 My son, forget not my law; but let thine heart keep my commandments: [2]For length of days, and long life, and peace, shall they add to thee. [3]Let not mercy and truth forsake thee: bind them about thy neck; write them upon the table of thine heart: [4]So shalt thou find favour and good understanding in the sight of God and man.

[5]Trust in the LORD with all thine heart; and lean not unto thine own understanding. [6]In all thy ways acknowledge him, and he shall direct thy paths.

[7]Be not wise in thine own eyes: fear the LORD, and depart from evil. [8]It shall be health to thy navel, and marrow to thy bones. [9]Honour the LORD with thy substance, and with the firstfruits of all thine increase: [10]So shall thy barns be filled with plenty, and thy presses shall burst out with new wine.

[11]My son, despise not the chastening of the LORD; neither be weary of his correction: [12]For whom the LORD loveth he correcteth; even as a father the son *in whom* he delighteth.

[13]Happy *is* the man *that* findeth wisdom, and the man *that* getteth understanding. [14]For the merchandise of it *is* better than the merchandise of silver, and the gain thereof than fine

gold. [15]She *is* more precious than rubies: and all the things thou canst desire are not to be compared unto her. [16]Length of days *is* in her right hand; *and* in her left hand riches and honour. [17]Her ways *are* ways of pleasantness, and all her paths *are* peace. [18]She *is* a tree of life to them that lay hold upon her: and happy *is every one* that retaineth her. [19]The LORD by wisdom hath founded the earth; by understanding hath he established the heavens. [20]By his knowledge the depths are broken up, and the clouds drop down the dew.

[21]My son, let not them depart from thine eyes: keep sound wisdom and discretion: [22]So shall they be life unto thy soul, and grace to thy neck. [23]Then shalt thou walk in thy way safely, and thy foot shall not stumble. [24]When thou liest down, thou shalt not be afraid: yea, thou shalt lie down, and thy sleep shall be sweet. [25]Be not afraid of sudden fear, neither of the desolation of the wicked, when it cometh. [26]For the LORD shall be thy confidence, and shall keep thy foot from being taken.

[27]Withhold not good from them to whom it is due, when it is in the power of thine hand to do *it*. [28]Say not unto thy neighbour, Go, and come again, and to morrow I will give; when thou hast it by thee. [29]Devise not evil against thy neighbour, seeing he dwelleth securely by thee.

[30]Strive not with a man without cause, if he have done thee no harm.

[31]Envy thou not the oppressor, and choose none of his ways. [32]For the froward *is* abomination to the LORD: but his secret *is* with the righteous.

[33]The curse of the LORD *is* in the house of the wicked: but he blesseth the habitation of the just. [34]Surely he scorneth the scorners: but he giveth grace unto the lowly. [35]The wise shall inherit glory: but shame shall be the promotion of fools.

4 Hear, ye children, the instruction of a father, and attend to know understanding. [2]For I give you good doctrine, forsake ye not my law. [3]For I was my father's son, tender and only *beloved* in the sight of my mother. [4]He taught me also, and said unto me, Let thine heart retain my words: keep my commandments, and live. [5]Get wisdom, get understanding: forget *it* not; neither decline from the words of my mouth. [6]Forsake her not, and she shall preserve thee: love her, and she shall keep thee. [7]Wisdom *is* the principal thing; *therefore* get wisdom: and with all thy getting get understanding. [8]Exalt her, and she shall promote thee: she shall bring thee to honour, when thou dost embrace her. [9]She shall give to thine head an ornament of grace: a crown of glory shall she deliver to thee. [10]Hear, O my son, and receive my sayings; and the years of thy life shall be many. [11]I have taught thee in the way of wisdom; I have led thee in right paths. [12]When thou goest, thy steps shall not be straitened; and when thou runnest, thou shalt not stumble. [13]Take fast hold of instruction; let *her* not go: keep her; for she *is* thy life.

¹⁴Enter not into the path of the wicked, and go not in the way of evil *men.* ¹⁵Avoid it, pass not by it, turn from it, and pass away. ¹⁶For they sleep not, except they have done mischief; and their sleep is taken away, unless they cause *some* to fall. ¹⁷For they eat the bread of wickedness, and drink the wine of violence. ¹⁸But the path of the just *is* as the shining light, that shineth more and more unto the perfect day. ¹⁹The way of the wicked *is* as darkness: they know not at what they stumble.

²⁰My son, attend to my words; incline thine ear unto my sayings. ²¹Let them not depart from thine eyes; keep them in the midst of thine heart. ²²For they *are* life unto those that find them, and health to all their flesh.

²³Keep thy heart with all diligence; for out of it *are* the issues of life. ²⁴Put away from thee a froward mouth, and perverse lips put far from thee. ²⁵Let thine eyes look right on, and let thine eyelids look straight before thee. ²⁶Ponder the path of thy feet, and let all thy ways be established. ²⁷Turn not to the right hand nor to the left: remove thy foot from evil.

5 My son, attend unto my wisdom, *and* bow thine ear to my understanding: ²That thou mayest regard discretion, and *that* thy lips may keep knowledge.

³For the lips of a strange woman drop *as* an honeycomb, and her mouth *is* smoother than oil: ⁴But her end is bitter as wormwood, sharp as a twoedged sword. ⁵Her feet go down to death; her steps take hold on hell. ⁶Lest thou shouldest ponder the path of life, her ways are moveable, *that* thou canst not know *them.* ⁷Hear me now therefore, O ye children, and depart not from the words of my mouth. ⁸Remove thy way far from her, and come not nigh the door of her house: ⁹Lest thou give thine honour unto others, and thy years unto the cruel: ¹⁰Lest strangers be filled with thy wealth; and thy labours *be* in the house of a stranger; ¹¹And thou mourn at the last, when thy flesh and thy body are consumed, ¹²And say, How have I hated instruction, and my heart despised reproof; ¹³And have not obeyed the voice of my teachers, nor inclined mine ear to them that instructed me! ¹⁴I was almost in all evil in the midst of the congregation and assembly.

¹⁵Drink waters out of thine own cistern, and running waters out of thine own well. ¹⁶Let thy fountains be dispersed abroad, *and* rivers of waters in the streets. ¹⁷Let them be only thine own, and not strangers' with thee. ¹⁸Let thy fountain be blessed: and rejoice with the wife of thy youth. ¹⁹*Let her be as* the loving hind and pleasant roe; let her breasts satisfy thee at all times; and be thou ravished always with her love. ²⁰And why wilt thou, my son, be ravished with a strange woman, and embrace the bosom of a stranger? ²¹For the ways of man *are* before the eyes of the LORD, and he pondereth all his goings.

²²His own iniquities shall take the wicked himself, and he shall be holden with the cords of his sins. ²³He shall die without instruction; and in the greatness of his folly he shall go astray.

6 My son, if thou be surety for thy friend, *if* thou hast stricken thy hand with a stranger, ²Thou art snared with the words of thy mouth, thou art taken with the words of thy mouth. ³Do this now, my son, deliver thyself, when thou art come into the hand of thy friend; go, humble thyself, and make sure thy friend. ⁴Give not sleep to thine eyes, nor slumber to thine eyelids. ⁵Deliver thyself as a roe from the hand *of the hunter,* and as a bird from the hand of the fowler.

⁶Go to the ant, thou sluggard; consider her ways, and be wise: ⁷Which having no guide, overseer, or ruler, ⁸Provideth her meat in the summer, *and* gathereth her food in the harvest. ⁹How long wilt thou sleep, O sluggard? when wilt thou arise out of thy sleep? ¹⁰*Yet* a little sleep, a little slumber, a little folding of the hands to sleep: ¹¹So shall thy poverty come as one that travelleth, and thy want as an armed man.

¹²A naughty person, a wicked man, walketh with a froward mouth. ¹³He winketh with his eyes, he speaketh with his feet, he teacheth with his fingers; ¹⁴Frowardness *is* in his heart, he deviseth mischief continually; he soweth discord. ¹⁵Therefore shall his calamity come suddenly; suddenly shall he be broken without remedy.

¹⁶These six *things* doth the LORD hate: yea, seven *are* an abomination unto him: ¹⁷A proud look, a lying tongue, and hands that shed innocent blood, ¹⁸An heart that deviseth wicked imaginations, feet that be swift in running to mischief, ¹⁹A false witness *that* speaketh lies, and he that soweth discord among brethren.

²⁰My son, keep thy father's commandment, and forsake not the law of thy mother: ²¹Bind them continually upon thine heart, *and* tie them about thy neck. ²²When thou goest, it shall lead thee; when thou sleepest, it shall keep thee; and *when* thou awakest, it shall talk with thee. ²³For the commandment *is* a lamp; and the law *is* light; and reproofs of instruction *are* the way of life: ²⁴To keep thee from the evil woman, from the flattery of the tongue of a strange woman. ²⁵Lust not after her beauty in thine heart; neither let her take thee with her eyelids. ²⁶For by means of a whorish woman *a man is brought* to a piece of bread: and the adulteress will hunt for the precious life. ²⁷Can a man take fire in his bosom, and his clothes not be burned? ²⁸Can one go upon hot coals, and his feet not be burned? ²⁹So he that goeth in to his neighbour's wife; whosoever toucheth her shall not be innocent. ³⁰*Men* do not despise a thief, if he steal to satisfy his soul when he is hungry; ³¹But *if* he be found, he shall restore sevenfold; he shall give all the substance of his house. ³²*But* whoso committeth adultery with a woman lacketh understanding: he *that* doeth it destroyeth his own soul. ³³A wound and dishonour shall he get; and his reproach shall not be wiped away. ³⁴For jealousy *is* the rage of

a man: therefore he will not spare in the day of vengeance. ³⁵He will not regard any ransom; neither will he rest content, though thou givest many gifts.

7 My son, keep my words, and lay up my commandments with thee. ²Keep my commandments, and live; and my law as the apple of thine eye. ³Bind them upon thy fingers, write them upon the table of thine heart. ⁴Say unto wisdom, Thou *art* my sister; and call understanding *thy* kinswoman: ⁵That they may keep thee from the strange woman, from the stranger *which* flattereth with her words.

⁶For at the window of my house I looked through my casement, ⁷And beheld among the simple ones, I discerned among the youths, a young man void of understanding, ⁸Passing through the street near her corner; and he went the way to her house, ⁹In the twilight, in the evening, in the black and dark night: ¹⁰And, behold, there met him a woman *with* the attire of an harlot, and subtil of heart. ¹¹(She *is* loud and stubborn; her feet abide not in her house: ¹²Now *is she* without, now in the streets, and lieth in wait at every corner.) ¹³So she caught him, and kissed him, *and* with an impudent face said unto him, ¹⁴*I have* peace offerings with me; this day have I payed my vows. ¹⁵Therefore came I forth to meet thee, diligently to seek thy face, and I have found thee. ¹⁶I have decked my bed with coverings of tapestry, with carved *works,* with fine linen of Egypt. ¹⁷I have perfumed my bed with myrrh, aloes, and cinnamon. ¹⁸Come, let us take our fill of love until the morning: let us solace ourselves with loves. ¹⁹For the goodman *is* not at home, he is gone a long journey: ²⁰He hath taken a bag of money with him, *and* will come home at the day appointed. ²¹With her much fair speech she caused him to yield, with the flattering of her lips she forced him. ²²He goeth after her straightway, as an ox goeth to the slaughter, or as a fool to the correction of the stocks; ²³Till a dart strike through his liver; as a bird hasteth to the snare, and knoweth not that it *is* for his life.

²⁴Hearken unto me now therefore, O ye children, and attend to the words of my mouth. ²⁵Let not thine heart decline to her ways, go not astray in her paths. ²⁶For she hath cast down many wounded: yea, many strong *men* have been slain by her. ²⁷Her house *is* the way to hell, going down to the chambers of death.

8 Doth not wisdom cry? and understanding put forth her voice? ²She standeth in the top of high places, by the way in the places of the paths. ³She crieth at the gates, at the entry of the city, at the coming in at the doors. ⁴Unto you, O men, I call; and my voice *is* to the sons of man. ⁵O ye simple, understand wisdom: and, ye fools, be ye of an understanding heart. ⁶Hear; for I will speak of excellent things; and the opening of my lips *shall be* right things. ⁷For my mouth shall speak truth; and wickedness *is* an abomination to my lips. ⁸All the words of my mouth *are* in righteousness; *there is* nothing froward or perverse in them. ⁹They *are* all plain to him that understandeth, and right to them that find knowledge. ¹⁰Receive my instruction, and not silver; and knowledge rather than

choice gold. [11]For wisdom *is* better than rubies; and all the things that may be desired are not to be compared to it. [12]I wisdom dwell with prudence, and find out knowledge of witty inventions. [13]The fear of the LORD *is* to hate evil: pride, and arrogancy, and the evil way, and the froward mouth, do I hate. [14]Counsel *is* mine, and sound wisdom: I *am* understanding; I have strength. [15]By me kings reign, and princes decree justice. [16]By me princes rule, and nobles, *even* all the judges of the earth. [17]I love them that love me; and those that seek me early shall find me. [18]Riches and honour *are* with me; *yea,* durable riches and righteousness. [19]My fruit *is* better than gold, yea, than fine gold; and my revenue than choice silver. [20]I lead in the way of righteousness, in the midst of the paths of judgment: [21]That I may cause those that love me to inherit substance; and I will fill their treasures. [22]The LORD possessed me in the beginning of his way, before his works of old. [23]I was set up from everlasting, from the beginning, or ever the earth was. [24]When *there were* no depths, I was brought forth; when *there were* no fountains abounding with water. [25]Before the mountains were settled, before the hills was I brought forth: [26]While as yet he had not made the earth, nor the fields, nor the highest part of the dust of the world. [27]When he prepared the heavens, I *was* there: when he set a compass upon the face of the depth: [28]When he established the clouds above: when he strengthened the fountains of the deep: [29]When he gave to the sea his decree, that the waters should not pass his commandment: when he appointed the foundations of the earth: [30]Then I was by him, *as* one brought up *with him:* and I was daily *his* delight, rejoicing always before him; [31]Rejoicing in the habitable part of his earth; and my delights *were* with the sons of men. [32]Now therefore hearken unto me, O ye children: for blessed *are they that* keep my ways. [33]Hear instruction, and be wise, and refuse it not. [34]Blessed *is* the man that heareth me, watching daily at my gates, waiting at the posts of my doors. [35]For whoso findeth me findeth life, and shall obtain favour of the LORD. [36]But he that sinneth against me wrongeth his own soul: all they that hate me love death.

9 Wisdom hath builded her house, she hath hewn out her seven pillars: [2]She hath killed her beasts; she hath mingled her wine; she hath also furnished her table. [3]She hath sent forth her maidens: she crieth upon the highest places of the city, [4]Whoso *is* simple, let him turn in hither: *as for* him that wanteth understanding, she saith to him, [5]Come, eat of my bread, and drink of the wine *which* I have mingled. [6]Forsake the foolish, and live; and go in the way of understanding. [7]He that reproveth a scorner getteth to himself shame: and he that rebuketh a wicked *man getteth* himself a blot. [8]Reprove not a scorner, lest he hate thee: rebuke a wise man, and he will love thee. [9]Give *instruction* to a wise *man,* and he will be yet wiser: teach a just *man,* and he will increase in learning. [10]The fear of the LORD *is* the beginning of wisdom: and the knowledge of the holy *is* understanding. [11]For by me thy days shall be multiplied, and the years of thy life shall be increased. [12]If thou be wise, thou shalt be wise for thyself: but *if* thou scornest, thou alone shalt bear *it.*

¹³A foolish woman *is* clamorous: *she is* simple, and knoweth nothing. ¹⁴For she sitteth at the door of her house, on a seat in the high places of the city, ¹⁵To call passengers who go right on their ways: ¹⁶Whoso *is* simple, let him turn in hither: and *as for* him that wanteth understanding, she saith to him, ¹⁷Stolen waters are sweet, and bread *eaten* in secret is pleasant. ¹⁸But he knoweth not that the dead *are* there; *and that* her guests *are* in the depths of hell.

10 The proverbs of Solomon. A wise son maketh a glad father: but a foolish son *is* the heaviness of his mother. ²Treasures of wickedness profit nothing: but righteousness delivereth from death. ³The LORD will not suffer the soul of the righteous to famish: but he casteth away the substance of the wicked. ⁴He becometh poor that dealeth *with* a slack hand: but the hand of the diligent maketh rich. ⁵He that gathereth in summer *is* a wise son: *but* he that sleepeth in harvest *is* a son that causeth shame. ⁶Blessings *are* upon the head of the just: but violence covereth the mouth of the wicked. ⁷The memory of the just is blessed: but the name of the wicked shall rot. ⁸The wise in heart will receive commandments: but a prating fool shall fall. ⁹He that walketh uprightly walketh surely: but he that perverteth his ways shall be known. ¹⁰He that winketh with the eye causeth sorrow: but a prating fool shall fall. ¹¹The mouth of a righteous *man is* a well of life: but violence covereth the mouth of the wicked. ¹²Hatred stirreth up strifes: but love covereth all sins. ¹³In the lips of him that hath understanding wisdom is found: but a rod *is* for the back of him that is void of understanding. ¹⁴Wise *men* lay up knowledge: but the mouth of the foolish *is* near destruction. ¹⁵The rich man's wealth *is* his strong city: the destruction of the poor *is* their poverty. ¹⁶The labour of the righteous *tendeth* to life: the fruit of the wicked to sin. ¹⁷He *is in* the way of life that keepeth instruction: but he that refuseth reproof erreth. ¹⁸He that hideth hatred *with* lying lips, and he that uttereth a slander, *is* a fool. ¹⁹In the multitude of words there wanteth not sin: but he that refraineth his lips *is* wise. ²⁰The tongue of the just *is as* choice silver: the heart of the wicked *is* little worth. ²¹The lips of the righteous feed many: but fools die for want of wisdom. ²²The blessing of the LORD, it maketh rich, and he addeth no sorrow with it. ²³*It is* as sport to a fool to do mischief: but a man of understanding hath wisdom. ²⁴The fear of the wicked, it shall come upon him: but the desire of the righteous shall be granted. ²⁵As the whirlwind passeth, so *is* the wicked no *more:* but the righteous *is* an everlasting foundation. ²⁶As vinegar to the teeth, and as smoke to the eyes, so *is* the sluggard to them that send him. ²⁷The fear of the LORD prolongeth days: but the years of the wicked shall be shortened. ²⁸The hope of the righteous *shall be* gladness: but the expectation of the wicked shall perish. ²⁹The way of the LORD *is* strength to the upright: but destruction *shall be* to the workers of iniquity. ³⁰The righteous shall never be removed: but the wicked shall not inhabit the earth. ³¹The mouth of the just bringeth forth wisdom: but the froward tongue shall be cut out. ³²The lips of the righteous know what is acceptable: but the mouth of the wicked *speaketh* frowardness.

11 A false balance *is* abomination to the LORD: but a just weight *is* his delight. [2]*When* pride cometh, then cometh shame: but with the lowly *is* wisdom. [3]The integrity of the upright shall guide them: but the perverseness of transgressors shall destroy them. [4]Riches profit not in the day of wrath: but righteousness delivereth from death. [5]The righteousness of the perfect shall direct his way: but the wicked shall fall by his own wickedness. [6]The righteousness of the upright shall deliver them: but transgressors shall be taken in *their own* naughtiness. [7]When a wicked man dieth, *his* expectation shall perish: and the hope of unjust *men* perisheth. [8]The righteous is delivered out of trouble, and the wicked cometh in his stead. [9]An hypocrite with *his* mouth destroyeth his neighbour: but through knowledge shall the just be delivered. [10]When it goeth well with the righteous, the city rejoiceth: and when the wicked perish, *there is* shouting. [11]By the blessing of the upright the city is exalted: but it is overthrown by the mouth of the wicked. [12]He that is void of wisdom despiseth his neighbour: but a man of understanding holdeth his peace. [13]A talebearer revealeth secrets: but he that is of a faithful spirit concealeth the matter. [14]Where no counsel *is,* the people fall: but in the multitude of counsellors *there is* safety. [15]He that is surety for a stranger shall smart *for it:* and he that hateth suretiship is sure. [16]A gracious woman retaineth honour: and strong *men* retain riches. [17]The merciful man doeth good to his own soul: but *he that is* cruel troubleth his own flesh. [18]The wicked worketh a deceitful work: but to him that soweth righteousness *shall be* a sure reward. [19]As righteousness *tendeth* to life: so he that pursueth evil *pursueth it* to his own death. [20]They that are of a froward heart *are* abomination to the LORD: but *such as are* upright in *their* way *are* his delight. [21]*Though* hand *join* in hand, the wicked shall not be unpunished: but the seed of the righteous shall be delivered. [22]*As* a jewel of gold in a swine's snout, *so is* a fair woman which is without discretion. [23]The desire of the righteous *is* only good: *but* the expectation of the wicked *is* wrath. [24]There is that scattereth, and yet increaseth; and *there is* that withholdeth more than is meet, but *it tendeth* to poverty. [25]The liberal soul shall be made fat: and he that watereth shall be watered also himself. [26]He that withholdeth corn, the people shall curse him: but blessing *shall be* upon the head of him that selleth *it.* [27]He that diligently seeketh good procureth favour: but he that seeketh mischief, it shall come unto him. [28]He that trusteth in his riches shall fall: but the righteous shall flourish as a branch. [29]He that troubleth his own house shall inherit the wind: and the fool *shall be* servant to the wise of heart. [30]The fruit of the righteous *is* a tree of life; and he that winneth souls *is* wise. [31]Behold, the righteous shall be recompensed in the earth: much more the wicked and the sinner.

12 Whoso loveth instruction loveth knowledge: but he that hateth reproof *is* brutish. [2]A good *man* obtaineth favour of the LORD: but a man of wicked devices will he condemn. [3]A man shall not be established by wickedness: but the root of the righteous shall not be moved. [4]A virtuous woman *is* a crown to her husband: but she that maketh ashamed *is* as rottenness in his bones. [5]The thoughts of the righteous *are* right: *but* the counsels of the wicked *are* deceit. [6]The words of the wicked *are* to lie in wait for blood: but the mouth of the upright shall deliver them. [7]The wicked are overthrown, and

are not: but the house of the righteous shall stand. [8]A man shall be commended according to his wisdom: but he that is of a perverse heart shall be despised. [9]*He that is* despised, and hath a servant, *is* better than he that honoureth himself, and lacketh bread. [10]A righteous *man* regardeth the life of his beast: but the tender mercies of the wicked *are* cruel. [11]He that tilleth his land shall be satisfied with bread: but he that followeth vain *persons is* void of understanding. [12]The wicked desireth the net of evil *men:* but the root of the righteous yieldeth *fruit.* [13]The wicked is snared by the transgression of *his* lips: but the just shall come out of trouble. [14]A man shall be satisfied with good by the fruit of *his* mouth: and the recompense of a man's hands shall be rendered unto him. [15]The way of a fool *is* right in his own eyes: but he that hearkeneth unto counsel *is* wise. [16]A fool's wrath is presently known: but a prudent *man* covereth shame. [17]*He that* speaketh truth sheweth forth righteousness: but a false witness deceit. [18]There is that speaketh like the piercings of a sword: but the tongue of the wise *is* health. [19]The lip of truth shall be established for ever: but a lying tongue *is* but for a moment. [20]Deceit *is* in the heart of them that imagine evil: but to the counsellors of peace *is* joy. [21]There shall no evil happen to the just: but the wicked shall be filled with mischief. [22]Lying lips *are* abomination to the LORD: but they that deal truly *are* his delight. [23]A prudent man concealeth knowledge: but the heart of fools proclaimeth foolishness. [24]The hand of the diligent shall bear rule: but the slothful shall be under tribute. [25]Heaviness in the heart of man maketh it stoop: but a good word maketh it glad. [26]The righteous *is* more excellent than his neighbour: but the way of the wicked seduceth them. [27]The slothful *man* roasteth not that which he took in hunting: but the substance of a diligent man *is* precious. [28]In the way of righteousness *is* life; and *in* the pathway *thereof there is* no death.

13

A wise son *heareth* his father's instruction: but a scorner heareth not rebuke. [2]A man shall eat good by the fruit of *his* mouth: but the soul of the transgressors *shall eat* violence. [3]He that keepeth his mouth keepeth his life: *but* he that openeth wide his lips shall have destruction. [4]The soul of the sluggard desireth, and *hath* nothing: but the soul of the diligent shall be made fat. [5]A righteous *man* hateth lying: but a wicked *man* is loathsome, and cometh to shame. [6]Righteousness keepeth *him that is* upright in the way: but wickedness overthroweth the sinner. [7]There is that maketh himself rich, yet *hath* nothing: *there is* that maketh himself poor, yet *hath* great riches. [8]The ransom of a man's life *are* his riches: but the poor heareth not rebuke. [9]The light of the righteous rejoiceth: but the lamp of the wicked shall be put out. [10]Only by pride cometh contention: but with the well advised *is* wisdom. [11]Wealth *gotten* by vanity shall be diminished: but he that gathereth by labour shall increase. [12]Hope deferred maketh the heart sick: but *when* the desire cometh, *it is* a tree of life. [13]Whoso despiseth the word shall be destroyed: but he that feareth the commandment shall be rewarded. [14]The law of the wise *is* a fountain of life, to depart from the snares of death. [15]Good understanding giveth favour: but the way of transgressors *is* hard. [16]Every prudent *man* dealeth with knowledge: but a fool layeth open *his* folly. [17]A wicked messenger falleth into mischief: but a faithful ambassador *is* health. [18]Poverty and shame *shall be to* him that refuseth instruction: but he that regardeth reproof shall be honoured. ¹⁹The desire accomplished is sweet to the soul: but *it is* abomination to fools to depart from evil. ²⁰He that walketh with wise *men* shall be wise: but a companion of fools shall be destroyed. ²¹Evil pursueth sinners: but to the righteous good shall be repaid. ²²A good *man* leaveth an inheritance to his children's children: and the wealth of the sinner is laid up for the just. ²³Much food *is in* the tillage of the poor: but there is *that is* destroyed for want of judgment. ²⁴He that spareth his rod hateth his son: but he that loveth him chasteneth him betimes. ²⁵The righteous eateth to the satisfying of his soul: but the belly of the wicked shall want.

14 Every wise woman buildeth her house: but the foolish plucketh it down with her hands. ²He that walketh in his uprightness feareth the LORD: but *he that is* perverse in his ways despiseth him. ³In the mouth of the foolish is a rod of pride: but the lips of the wise shall preserve them. ⁴Where no oxen *are,* the crib *is* clean: but much increase *is* by the strength of the ox. ⁵A faithful witness will not lie: but a false witness will utter lies. ⁶A scorner seeketh wisdom, and *findeth it* not: but knowledge *is* easy unto him that understandeth. ⁷Go from the presence of a foolish man, when thou perceivest not *in him* the lips of knowledge. ⁸The wisdom of the prudent *is* to understand his way: but the folly of fools *is* deceit. ⁹Fools make a mock at sin: but among the righteous *there is* favour. ¹⁰The heart knoweth his own bitterness; and a stranger doth not intermeddle with his joy. ¹¹The house of the wicked shall be overthrown: but the tabernacle of the upright shall flourish. ¹²There is a way which seemeth right unto a man, but the end thereof *are* the ways of death. ¹³Even in laughter the heart is sorrowful; and the end of that mirth *is* heaviness. ¹⁴The backslider in heart shall be filled with his own ways: and a good man *shall be satisfied* from himself. ¹⁵The simple believeth every word: but the prudent *man* looketh well to his going. ¹⁶A wise *man* feareth, and departeth from evil: but the fool rageth, and is confident. ¹⁷*He that is* soon angry dealeth foolishly: and a man of wicked devices is hated. ¹⁸The simple inherit folly: but the prudent are crowned with knowledge. ¹⁹The evil bow before the good; and the wicked at the gates of the righteous. ²⁰The poor is hated even of his own neighbour: but the rich *hath* many friends. ²¹He that despiseth his neighbour sinneth: but he that hath mercy on the poor, happy *is* he. ²²Do they not err that devise evil? but mercy and truth *shall be* to them that devise good. ²³In all labour there is profit: but the talk of the lips *tendeth* only to penury. ²⁴The crown of the wise is their riches: *but* the foolishness of fools *is* folly. ²⁵A true witness delivereth souls: but a deceitful *witness* speaketh lies. ²⁶In the fear of the LORD *is* strong confidence: and his children shall have a place of refuge. ²⁷The fear of the LORD *is* a fountain of life, to depart from the snares of death. ²⁸In the multitude of people *is* the king's honour: but in the want of people *is* the destruction of the prince. ²⁹He that is slow to wrath *is* of great understanding: but *he that is* hasty of spirit exalteth folly. ³⁰A sound heart *is* the life of the flesh: but envy the rottenness of the bones. ³¹He that oppresseth the poor reproacheth his Maker: but he that honoureth him hath mercy on the poor. ³²The wicked is driven away in his wickedness: but the righteous hath hope in his death. ³³Wisdom resteth in the heart of him that hath understanding: but *that which is* in the midst of fools is made known.

³⁴Righteousness exalteth a nation: but sin *is* a reproach to any people. ³⁵The king's favour *is* toward a wise servant: but his wrath is *against* him that causeth shame.

15 A soft answer turneth away wrath: but grievous words stir up anger. ²The tongue of the wise useth knowledge aright: but the mouth of fools poureth out foolishness. ³The eyes of the LORD *are* in every place, beholding the evil and the good. ⁴A wholesome tongue *is* a tree of life: but perverseness therein *is* a breach in the spirit. ⁵A fool despiseth his father's instruction: but he that regardeth reproof is prudent. ⁶In the house of the righteous *is* much treasure: but in the revenues of the wicked is trouble. ⁷The lips of the wise disperse knowledge: but the heart of the foolish *doeth* not so. ⁸The sacrifice of the wicked *is* an abomination to the LORD: but the prayer of the upright *is* his delight. ⁹The way of the wicked *is* an abomination unto the LORD: but he loveth him that followeth after righteousness. ¹⁰Correction *is* grievous unto him that forsaketh the way: *and* he that hateth reproof shall die. ¹¹Hell and destruction *are* before the LORD: how much more then the hearts of the children of men? ¹²A scorner loveth not one that reproveth him: neither will he go unto the wise. ¹³A merry heart maketh a cheerful countenance: but by sorrow of the heart the spirit is broken. ¹⁴The heart of him that hath understanding seeketh knowledge: but the mouth of fools feedeth on foolishness. ¹⁵All the days of the afflicted *are* evil: but he that is of a merry heart *hath* a continual feast. ¹⁶Better *is* little with the fear of the LORD than great treasure and trouble therewith. ¹⁷Better *is* a dinner of herbs where love is, than a stalled ox and hatred therewith. ¹⁸A wrathful man stirreth up strife: but *he that is* slow to anger appeaseth strife. ¹⁹The way of the slothful *man is* as an hedge of thorns: but the way of the righteous *is* made plain. ²⁰A wise son maketh a glad father: but a foolish man despiseth his mother. ²¹Folly *is* joy to *him that is* destitute of wisdom: but a man of understanding walketh uprightly. ²²Without counsel purposes are disappointed: but in the multitude of counsellors they are established. ²³A man hath joy by the answer of his mouth: and a word *spoken* in due season, how good *is it!* ²⁴The way of life *is* above to the wise, that he may depart from hell beneath. ²⁵The LORD will destroy the house of the proud: but he will establish the border of the widow. ²⁶The thoughts of the wicked *are* an abomination to the LORD: but *the words* of the pure *are* pleasant words. ²⁷He that is greedy of gain troubleth his own house; but he that hateth gifts shall live. ²⁸The heart of the righteous studieth to answer: but the mouth of the wicked poureth out evil things. ²⁹The LORD *is* far from the wicked: but he heareth the prayer of the righteous. ³⁰The light of the eyes rejoiceth the heart: *and* a good report maketh the bones fat. ³¹The ear that heareth the reproof of life abideth among the wise. ³²He that refuseth instruction despiseth his own soul: but he that heareth reproof getteth understanding. ³³The fear of the LORD *is* the instruction of wisdom; and before honour *is* humility.

16 The preparations of the heart in man, and the answer of the tongue, *is* from the LORD. ²All the ways of a man *are* clean in his own eyes; but the LORD weigheth the spirits. ³Commit thy works unto the LORD, and thy thoughts shall be established. ⁴The LORD hath made all *things* for himself: yea, even the wicked for the day of evil. ⁵Every one *that is* proud in heart *is* an abomination to the LORD: *though* hand *join* in hand, he shall not be unpunished. ⁶By mercy and truth iniquity is purged: and by the fear of the LORD *men* depart from evil. ⁷When a man's ways please the LORD, he maketh even his enemies to be at peace with him. ⁸Better *is* a little with righteousness than great revenues without right. ⁹A man's heart deviseth his way: but the LORD directeth his steps. ¹⁰A divine sentence *is* in the lips of the king: his mouth transgresseth not in judgment. ¹¹A just weight and balance *are* the LORD'S: all the weights of the bag *are* his work. ¹²*It is* an abomination to kings to commit wickedness: for the throne is established by righteousness. ¹³Righteous lips *are* the delight of kings; and they love him that speaketh right. ¹⁴The wrath of a king *is as* messengers of death: but a wise man will pacify it. ¹⁵In the light of the king's countenance *is* life; and his favour *is* as a cloud of the latter rain. ¹⁶How much better *is it* to get wisdom than gold! and to get understanding rather to be chosen than silver! ¹⁷The highway of the upright *is* to depart from evil: he that keepeth his way preserveth his soul. ¹⁸Pride *goeth* before destruction, and an haughty spirit before a fall. ¹⁹Better *it is to be* of an humble spirit with the lowly, than to divide the spoil with the proud. ²⁰He that handleth a matter wisely shall find good: and whoso trusteth in the LORD, happy *is* he. ²¹The wise in heart shall be called prudent: and the sweetness of the lips increaseth learning. ²²Understanding *is* a wellspring of life unto him that hath it: but the instruction of fools *is* folly. ²³The heart of the wise teacheth his mouth, and addeth learning to his lips. ²⁴Pleasant words *are as* an honeycomb, sweet to the soul, and health to the bones. ²⁵There is a way that seemeth right unto a man, but the end thereof *are* the ways of death. ²⁶He that laboureth laboureth for himself; for his mouth craveth it of him. ²⁷An ungodly man diggeth up evil: and in his lips *there is* as a burning fire. ²⁸A froward man soweth strife: and a whisperer separateth chief friends. ²⁹A violent man enticeth his neighbour, and leadeth him into the way *that is* not good. ³⁰He shutteth his eyes to devise froward things: moving his lips he bringeth evil to pass. ³¹The hoary head *is* a crown of glory, *if* it be found in the way of righteousness. ³²*He that is* slow to anger *is* better than the mighty; and he that ruleth his spirit than he that taketh a city. ³³The lot is cast into the lap; but the whole disposing thereof *is* of the LORD.

17 Better *is* a dry morsel, and quietness therewith, than an house full of sacrifices *with* strife. ²A wise servant shall have rule over a son that causeth shame, and shall have part of the inheritance among the brethren. ³The fining pot *is* for silver, and the furnace for gold: but the LORD trieth the hearts. ⁴A wicked doer giveth heed to false lips; *and* a liar giveth ear to a naughty tongue. ⁵Whoso mocketh the poor reproacheth his Maker: *and* he that is glad at calamities shall not be unpunished. ⁶Children's children *are* the crown of old men; and the glory of children *are* their fathers. ⁷Excellent speech becometh not a fool: much less do lying lips a prince. ⁸A gift *is as* a precious stone in the eyes of him that hath it: whithersoever it turneth, it prospereth. ⁹He that covereth a transgression seeketh love; but he that repeateth a matter separateth *very* friends. ¹⁰A reproof entereth more into a wise man than an hundred stripes into a fool. ¹¹An evil *man* seeketh only rebellion: therefore a cruel messenger shall be sent against him. ¹²Let a bear robbed of her whelps meet a man, rather than a fool in his folly. [13]Whoso rewardeth evil for good, evil shall not depart from his house. [14]The beginning of strife *is as* when one letteth out water: therefore leave off contention, before it be meddled with. [15]He that justifieth the wicked, and he that condemneth the just, even they both *are* abomination to the LORD. [16]Wherefore *is there* a price in the hand of a fool to get wisdom, seeing *he hath* no heart *to it?* [17]A friend loveth at all times, and a brother is born for adversity. [18]A man void of understanding striketh hands, *and* becometh surety in the presence of his friend. [19]He loveth transgression that loveth strife: *and* he that exalteth his gate seeketh destruction. [20]He that hath a froward heart findeth no good: and he that hath a perverse tongue falleth into mischief. [21]He that begetteth a fool *doeth it* to his sorrow: and the father of a fool hath no joy. [22]A merry heart doeth good *like* a medicine: but a broken spirit drieth the bones. [23]A wicked *man* taketh a gift out of the bosom to pervert the ways of judgment. [24]Wisdom *is* before him that hath understanding; but the eyes of a fool *are* in the ends of the earth. [25]A foolish son *is* a grief to his father, and bitterness to her that bare him. [26]Also to punish the just *is* not good, *nor* to strike princes for equity. [27]He that hath knowledge spareth his words: *and* a man of understanding is of an excellent spirit. [28]Even a fool, when he holdeth his peace, is counted wise: *and* he that shutteth his lips *is esteemed* a man of understanding.

18

Through desire a man, having separated himself, seeketh *and* intermeddleth with all wisdom. [2]A fool hath no delight in understanding, but that his heart may discover itself. [3]When the wicked cometh, *then* cometh also contempt, and with ignominy reproach. [4]The words of a man's mouth *are as* deep waters, *and* the wellspring of wisdom *as* a flowing brook. [5]*It is* not good to accept the person of the wicked, to overthrow the righteous in judgment. [6]A fool's lips enter into contention, and his mouth calleth for strokes. [7]A fool's mouth *is* his destruction, and his lips *are* the snare of his soul. [8]The words of a talebearer *are* as wounds, and they go down into the innermost parts of the belly. [9]He also that is slothful in his work is brother to him that is a great waster. [10]The name of the LORD *is* a strong tower: the righteous runneth into it, and is safe. [11]The rich man's wealth *is* his strong city, and as an high wall in his own conceit. [12]Before destruction the heart of man is haughty, and before honour *is* humility. [13]He that answereth a matter before he heareth *it,* it *is* folly and shame unto him. [14]The spirit of a man will sustain his infirmity; but a wounded spirit who can bear? [15]The heart of the prudent getteth knowledge; and the ear of the wise seeketh knowledge. [16]A man's gift maketh room for him, and bringeth him before great men. [17]*He that is* first in his own cause *seemeth* just; but his neighbour cometh and searcheth him. [18]The lot causeth contentions to cease, and parteth between the mighty. [19]A brother offended *is harder to be won* than a strong city: and *their* contentions *are* like the bars of a castle. [20]A man's belly shall be satisfied with the fruit of his mouth; *and* with the increase of his lips shall he be filled. [21]Death and life *are* in the power of the tongue: and they that love it shall eat the fruit thereof. [22]*Whoso* findeth a wife findeth a good *thing,* and obtaineth favour of the LORD. [23]The poor useth intreaties; but the rich answereth roughly. [24]A man *that hath* friends must shew himself friendly: and there is a friend *that* sticketh closer than a brother.

132

19 Better *is* the poor that walketh in his integrity, than *he that is* perverse in his lips, and is a fool. ²Also, *that* the soul *be* without knowledge, *it is* not good; and he that hasteth with *his* feet sinneth. ³The foolishness of man perverteth his way: and his heart fretteth against the LORD. ⁴Wealth maketh many friends; but the poor is separated from his neighbour. ⁵A false witness shall not be unpunished, and *he that* speaketh lies shall not escape. ⁶Many will intreat the favour of the prince: and every man *is* a friend to him that giveth gifts. ⁷All the brethren of the poor do hate him: how much more do his friends go far from him? he pursueth *them with* words, *yet* they *are* wanting *to him.* ⁸He that getteth wisdom loveth his own soul: *he that* keepeth understanding shall find good. ⁹A false witness shall not be unpunished, and he that speaketh lies shall perish. ¹⁰Delight is not seemly for a fool; much less for a servant to have rule over princes. ¹¹The discretion of a man deferreth his anger; and *it is* his glory to pass over a transgression. ¹²The king's wrath *is* as the roaring of a lion; but his favour *is* as dew upon the grass. ¹³A foolish son *is* the calamity of his father: and the contentions of a wife *are* a continual dropping. ¹⁴House and riches *are* the inheritance of fathers and a prudent wife *is* from the LORD. ¹⁵Slothfulness casteth into a deep sleep; and an idle soul shall suffer hunger. ¹⁶He that keepeth the commandment keepeth his own soul; *but* he that despiseth his ways shall die. ¹⁷He that hath pity upon the poor lendeth unto the LORD; and that which he hath given will he pay him again. ¹⁸Chasten thy son while there is hope, and let not thy soul spare for his crying. ¹⁹A man of great wrath shall suffer punishment: for if thou deliver *him,* yet thou must do it again. ²⁰Hear counsel, and receive instruction, that thou mayest be wise in thy latter end. ²¹*There are* many devices in a man's heart; nevertheless the counsel of the LORD, that shall stand. ²²The desire of a man *is* his kindness: and a poor man *is* better than a liar. ²³The fear of the LORD *tendeth* to life: and *he that hath it* shall abide satisfied; he shall not be visited with evil. ²⁴A slothful *man* hideth his hand in *his* bosom, and will not so much as bring it to his mouth again. ²⁵Smite a scorner, and the simple will beware: and reprove one that hath understanding, *and* he will understand knowledge. ²⁶He that wasteth *his* father, *and* chaseth away *his* mother, *is* a son that causeth shame, and bringeth reproach. ²⁷Cease, my son, to hear the instruction *that causeth* to err from the words of knowledge. ²⁸An ungodly witness scorneth judgment: and the mouth of the wicked devoureth iniquity. ²⁹Judgments are prepared for scorners, and stripes for the back of fools.

20 Wine *is* a mocker, strong drink *is* raging: and whosoever is deceived thereby is not wise. ²The fear of a king *is* as the roaring of a lion: *whoso* provoketh him to anger sinneth *against* his own soul. ³*It is* an honour for a man to cease from strife: but every fool will be meddling. ⁴The sluggard will not plow by reason of the cold; *therefore* shall he beg in harvest, and *have* nothing. ⁵Counsel in the heart of man *is like* deep water; but a man of understanding will draw it out. ⁶Most men will proclaim every one his own goodness: but a faithful man who can find? ⁷The just *man* walketh in his integrity: his children *are* blessed after him. ⁸A king that sitteth in the throne of judgment scattereth away all evil with his eyes. ⁹Who can say, I have made my heart clean, I am pure from my sin? ¹⁰Divers weights, *and* divers measures, both of them *are* alike abomination to the LORD. ¹¹Even a child is known by his doings, whether his work *be* pure, and whether *it be* right. ¹²The hearing ear, and the seeing eye, the LORD hath made even both of them. ¹³Love not sleep, lest thou come to poverty; open thine eyes, *and* thou shalt be satisfied with bread. ¹⁴*It is* naught, *it is* naught, saith the buyer: but when he is gone his way, then he boasteth. ¹⁵There is gold, and a multitude of rubies: but the lips of knowledge *are* a precious jewel. ¹⁶Take his garment that is surety *for* a stranger: and take a pledge of him for a strange woman. ¹⁷Bread of deceit *is* sweet to a man; but afterwards his mouth shall be filled with gravel. ¹⁸*Every* purpose is established by counsel: and with good advice make war. ¹⁹He that goeth about *as* a talebearer revealeth secrets: therefore meddle not with him that flattereth with his lips. ²⁰Whoso curseth his father or his mother, his lamp shall be put out in obscure darkness. ²¹An inheritance *may be* gotten hastily at the beginning; but the end thereof shall not be blessed. ²²Say not thou, I will recompense evil; *but* wait on the LORD, and he shall save thee. ²³Divers weights *are* an abomination unto the LORD; and a false balance *is* not good. ²⁴Man's goings *are* of the LORD; how can a man then understand his own way? ²⁵*It is* a snare to the man *who* devoureth *that which is* holy, and after vows to make enquiry. ²⁶A wise king scattereth the wicked, and bringeth the wheel over them. ²⁷The spirit of man *is* the candle of the LORD, searching all the inward parts of the belly. ²⁸Mercy and truth preserve the king: and his throne is upholden by mercy. ²⁹The glory of young men *is* their strength: and the beauty of old men *is* the grey head. ³⁰The blueness of a wound cleanseth away evil: so *do* stripes the inward parts of the belly.

21

The king's heart *is* in the hand of the LORD, *as* the rivers of water: he turneth it whithersoever he will. ²Every way of a man *is* right in his own eyes: but the LORD pondereth the hearts. ³To do justice and judgment *is* more acceptable to the LORD than sacrifice. ⁴An high look, and a proud heart, *and* the plowing of the wicked, *is* sin. ⁵The thoughts of the diligent *tend* only to plenteousness; but of every one *that is* hasty only to want. ⁶The getting of treasures by a lying tongue *is* a vanity tossed to and fro of them that seek death. ⁷The robbery of the wicked shall destroy them; because they refuse to do judgment. ⁸The way of man *is* froward and strange: but *as for* the pure, his work *is* right. ⁹*It is* better to dwell in a corner of the housetop, than with a brawling woman in a wide house. ¹⁰The soul of the wicked desireth evil: his neighbour findeth no favour in his eyes. ¹¹When the scorner is punished, the simple is made wise: and when the wise is instructed, he receiveth knowledge. ¹²The righteous *man* wisely considereth the house of the wicked: *but* God overthroweth the wicked for *their* wickedness. ¹³Whoso stoppeth his ears at the cry of the poor, he also shall cry himself, but shall not be heard. ¹⁴A gift in secret pacifieth anger: and a reward in the bosom strong wrath. ¹⁵*It is* joy to the just to do judgment: but destruction *shall be* to the workers of iniquity. ¹⁶The man that wandereth out of the way of understanding shall remain in the congregation of the dead. ¹⁷He that loveth pleasure *shall be* a poor man: he that loveth wine and oil shall not be rich. ¹⁸The wicked *shall be* a ransom for the righteous, and the transgressor for the upright. ¹⁹*It is* better to dwell in the wilderness, than with a contentious and an angry woman. ^{20}*There is* treasure to be desired and oil in the dwelling of the wise; but a foolish man spendeth it up. ^{21}He that followeth after righteousness and mercy findeth life, righteousness, and honour. ^{22}A wise *man* scaleth the city of the mighty, and casteth down the strength of the confidence thereof. ^{23}Whoso keepeth his mouth and his tongue keepeth his soul from troubles. ^{24}Proud *and* haughty scorner *is* his name, who dealeth in proud wrath. ^{25}The desire of the slothful killeth him; for his hands refuse to labour. ^{26}He coveteth greedily all the day long: but the righteous giveth and spareth not. ^{27}The sacrifice of the wicked *is* abomination: how much more, *when* he bringeth it with a wicked mind? ^{28}A false witness shall perish: but the man that heareth speaketh constantly. ^{29}A wicked man hardeneth his face: but *as for* the upright, he directeth his way. ^{30}*There is* no wisdom nor understanding nor counsel against the LORD. ^{31}The horse *is* prepared against the day of battle: but safety *is* of the LORD.

22 A *good* name *is* rather to be chosen than great riches, *and* loving favour rather than silver and gold. ^{2}The rich and poor meet together: the LORD *is* the maker of them all. ^{3}A prudent *man* foreseeth the evil, and hideth himself: but the simple pass on, and are punished. ^{4}By humility *and* the fear of the LORD *are* riches, and honour, and life. ^{5}Thorns *and* snares *are* in the way of the froward: he that doth keep his soul shall be far from them. ^{6}Train up a child in the way he should go: and when he is old, he will not depart from it. ^{7}The rich ruleth over the poor, and the borrower *is* servant to the lender. ^{8}He that soweth iniquity shall reap vanity: and the rod of his anger shall fail. ^{9}He that hath a bountiful eye shall be blessed; for he giveth of his bread to the poor. ^{10}Cast out the scorner, and contention shall go out; yea, strife and reproach shall cease. ^{11}He that loveth pureness of heart, *for* the grace of his lips the king *shall be* his friend. ^{12}The eyes of the LORD preserve knowledge, and he overthroweth the words of the transgressor. ^{13}The slothful *man* saith, *There is* a lion without, I shall be slain in the streets. ^{14}The mouth of strange women *is* a deep pit: he that is abhorred of the LORD shall fall therein. ^{15}Foolishness *is* bound in the heart of a child; *but* the rod of correction shall drive it far from him. ^{16}He that oppresseth the poor to increase his *riches, and* he that giveth to the rich, *shall* surely *come* to want. ^{17}Bow down thine ear, and hear the words of the wise, and apply thine heart unto my knowledge. ^{18}For *it is* a pleasant thing if thou keep them within thee; they shall withal be fitted in thy lips. ^{19}That thy trust may be in the LORD, I have made known to thee this day, even to thee. ^{20}Have not I written to thee excellent things in counsels and knowledge, ^{21}That I might make thee know the certainty of the words of truth; that thou mightest answer the words of truth to them that send unto thee? ^{22}Rob not the poor, because he *is* poor: neither oppress the afflicted in the gate: ^{23}For the LORD will plead their cause, and spoil the soul of those that spoiled them. ^{24}Make no friendship with an angry man; and with a furious man thou shalt not go: ^{25}Lest thou learn his ways, and get a snare to thy soul. ^{26}Be not thou *one* of them that strike hands, *or* of them that are sureties for debts. ^{27}If thou hast nothing to pay, why should he take away thy bed from under thee? ^{28}Remove not the ancient landmark, which thy fathers have set. ^{29}Seest thou a man diligent in his business? he shall stand before kings; he shall not stand before mean *men.*

23 When thou sittest to eat with a ruler, consider diligently what *is* before thee: ²And put a knife to thy throat, if thou *be* a man given to appetite. ³Be not desirous of his dainties: for they *are* deceitful meat. ⁴Labour not to be rich: cease from thine own wisdom. ⁵Wilt thou set thine eyes upon that which is not? for *riches* certainly make themselves wings; they fly away as an eagle toward heaven. ⁶Eat thou not the bread of *him that hath* an evil eye, neither desire thou his dainty meats: ⁷For as he thinketh in his heart, so *is* he: Eat and drink, saith he to thee; but his heart *is* not with thee. ⁸The morsel *which* thou hast eaten shalt thou vomit up, and lose thy sweet words. ⁹Speak not in the ears of a fool: for he will despise the wisdom of thy words. ¹⁰Remove not the old landmark; and enter not into the fields of the fatherless: ¹¹For their redeemer *is* mighty; he shall plead their cause with thee. ¹²Apply thine heart unto instruction, and thine ears to the words of knowledge. ¹³Withhold not correction from the child: for *if* thou beatest him with the rod, he shall not die. ¹⁴Thou shalt beat him with the rod, and shalt deliver his soul from hell. ¹⁵My son, if thine heart be wise, my heart shall rejoice, even mine. ¹⁶Yea, my reins shall rejoice, when thy lips speak right things. ¹⁷Let not thine heart envy sinners: but *be thou* in the fear of the LORD all the day long. ¹⁸For surely there is an end; and thine expectation shall not be cut off. ¹⁹Hear thou, my son, and be wise, and guide thine heart in the way. ²⁰Be not among winebibbers; among riotous eaters of flesh: ²¹For the drunkard and the glutton shall come to poverty: and drowsiness shall clothe *a man* with rags. ²²Hearken unto thy father that begat thee, and despise not thy mother when she is old. ²³Buy the truth, and sell *it* not; *also* wisdom, and instruction, and understanding. ²⁴The father of the righteous shall greatly rejoice: and he that begetteth a wise *child* shall have joy of him. ²⁵Thy father and thy mother shall be glad, and she that bare thee shall rejoice. ²⁶My son, give me thine heart, and let thine eyes observe my ways. ²⁷For a whore *is* a deep ditch; and a strange woman *is* a narrow pit. ²⁸She also lieth in wait as *for* a prey, and increaseth the transgressors among men. ²⁹Who hath woe? who hath sorrow? who hath contentions? who hath babbling? who hath wounds without cause? who hath redness of eyes? ³⁰They that tarry long at the wine; they that go to seek mixed wine. ³¹Look not thou upon the wine when it is red, when it giveth his colour in the cup, *when* it moveth itself aright. ³²At the last it biteth like a serpent, and stingeth like an adder. ³³Thine eyes shall behold strange women, and thine heart shall utter perverse things. ³⁴Yea, thou shalt be as he that lieth down in the midst of the sea, or as he that lieth upon the top of a mast. ³⁵They have stricken me, *shalt thou say, and* I was not sick; they have beaten me, *and* I felt *it* not: when shall I awake? I will seek it yet again.

24 Be not thou envious against evil men, neither desire to be with them. ²For their heart studieth destruction, and their lips talk of mischief. ³Through wisdom is an house builded; and by understanding it is established: ⁴And by knowledge shall the chambers be filled with all precious and pleasant riches. ⁵A wise man *is*

strong; yea, a man of knowledge increaseth strength. [6]For by wise counsel thou shalt make thy war: and in multitude of counsellors *there is* safety. [7]Wisdom *is* too high for a fool: he openeth not his mouth in the gate. [8]He that deviseth to do evil shall be called a mischievous person. [9]The thought of foolishness *is* sin: and the scorner *is* an abomination to men. [10]*If* thou faint in the day of adversity, thy strength *is* small. [11]If thou forbear to deliver *them that are* drawn unto death, and *those that are* ready to be slain; [12]If thou sayest, Behold, we knew it not; doth not he that pondereth the heart consider *it?* and he that keepeth thy soul, doth *not* he know *it?* and shall *not* he render to *every* man according to his works? [13]My son, eat thou honey, because *it is* good; and the honeycomb, *which is* sweet to thy taste: [14]So *shall* the knowledge of wisdom *be* unto thy soul: when thou hast found *it,* then there shall be a reward, and thy expectation shall not be cut off. [15]Lay not wait, O wicked *man,* against the dwelling of the righteous; spoil not his resting place: [16]For a just *man* falleth seven times, and riseth up again: but the wicked shall fall into mischief. [17]Rejoice not when thine enemy falleth, and let not thine heart be glad when he stumbleth: [18]Lest the LORD see *it,* and it displease him, and he turn away his wrath from him. [19]Fret not thyself because of evil *men,* neither be thou envious at the wicked; [20]For there shall be no reward to the evil *man;* the candle of the wicked shall be put out. [21]My son, fear thou the LORD and the king: *and* meddle not with them that are given to change: [22]For their calamity shall rise suddenly; and who knoweth the ruin of them both? [23]These *things* also *belong* to the wise. *It is* not good to have respect of persons in judgment. [24]He that saith unto the wicked, Thou *art* righteous; him shall the people curse, nations shall abhor him: [25]But to them that rebuke *him* shall be delight, and a good blessing shall come upon them. [26]*Every man* shall kiss *his* lips that giveth a right answer. [27]Prepare thy work without, and make it fit for thyself in the field; and afterwards build thine house. [28]Be not a witness against thy neighbour without cause; and deceive *not* with thy lips. [29]Say not, I will do so to him as he hath done to me: I will render to the man according to his work. [30]I went by the field of the slothful, and by the vineyard of the man void of understanding; [31]And, lo, it was all grown over with thorns, *and* nettles had covered the face thereof, and the stone wall thereof was broken down. [32]Then I saw, *and* considered *it* well: I looked upon *it, and* received instruction. [33]*Yet* a little sleep, a little slumber, a little folding of the hands to sleep: [34]So shall thy poverty come as one that travelleth; and thy want as an armed man.

25

These *are* also proverbs of Solomon, which the men of Hezekiah king of Judah copied out. [2]*It is* the glory of God to conceal a thing: but the honour of kings *is* to search out a matter. [3]The heaven for height, and the earth for depth, and the heart of kings *is* unsearchable. [4]Take away the dross from the silver, and there shall come forth a vessel for the finer. [5]Take away the wicked *from* before the king, and his throne shall be established in righteousness. [6]Put not forth thyself in the presence of the king, and stand not in the place of great *men:* [7]For better *it is* that it be said unto thee, Come up hither; than that thou shouldest be put lower in the presence of the prince whom thine eyes have seen. [8]Go not forth hastily to strive, lest *thou know not* what to do in the end thereof, when thy neighbour hath put thee to shame. ⁹Debate thy cause with thy neighbour *himself;* and discover not a secret to another: ¹⁰Lest he that heareth *it* put thee to shame, and thine infamy turn not away. ¹¹A word fitly spoken *is like* apples of gold in pictures of silver. ¹²*As* an earring of gold, and an ornament of fine gold, *so is* a wise reprover upon an obedient ear. ¹³As the cold of snow in the time of harvest, *so is* a faithful messenger to them that send him: for he refresheth the soul of his masters. ¹⁴Whoso boasteth himself of a false gift *is like* clouds and wind without rain. ¹⁵By long forbearing is a prince persuaded, and a soft tongue breaketh the bone. ¹⁶Hast thou found honey? eat so much as is sufficient for thee, lest thou be filled therewith, and vomit it. ¹⁷Withdraw thy foot from thy neighbour's house; lest he be weary of thee, and *so* hate thee. ¹⁸A man that beareth false witness against his neighbour *is* a maul, and a sword, and a sharp arrow. ¹⁹Confidence in an unfaithful man in time of trouble *is like* a broken tooth, and a foot out of joint. ²⁰*As* he that taketh away a garment in cold weather, *and as* vinegar upon nitre, so *is* he that singeth songs to an heavy heart. ²¹If thine enemy be hungry, give him bread to eat; and if he be thirsty, give him water to drink: ²²For thou shalt heap coals of fire upon his head, and the LORD shall reward thee. ²³The north wind driveth away rain: so *doth* an angry countenance a backbiting tongue. ²⁴*It is* better to dwell in the corner of the housetop, than with a brawling woman and in a wide house. ²⁵*As* cold waters to a thirsty soul, so *is* good news from a far country. ²⁶A righteous man falling down before the wicked *is as* a troubled fountain, and a corrupt spring. ²⁷*It is* not good to eat much honey: so *for men* to search their own glory *is not* glory. ²⁸He that *hath* no rule over his own spirit *is like* a city *that is* broken down, *and* without walls.

26 As snow in summer, and as rain in harvest, so honour is not seemly for a fool. ²As the bird by wandering, as the swallow by flying, so the curse causeless shall not come. ³A whip for the horse, a bridle for the ass, and a rod for the fool's back. ⁴Answer not a fool according to his folly, lest thou also be like unto him. ⁵Answer a fool according to his folly, lest he be wise in his own conceit. ⁶He that sendeth a message by the hand of a fool cutteth off the feet, *and* drinketh damage. ⁷The legs of the lame are not equal: so *is* a parable in the mouth of fools. ⁸As he that bindeth a stone in a sling, so *is* he that giveth honour to a fool. ⁹*As* a thorn goeth up into the hand of a drunkard, so *is* a parable in the mouth of fools. ¹⁰The great *God* that formed all *things* both rewardeth the fool, and rewardeth transgressors. ¹¹As a dog returneth to his vomit, *so* a fool returneth to his folly. ¹²Seest thou a man wise in his own conceit? *there is* more hope of a fool than of him. ¹³The slothful *man* saith, *There is* a lion in the way; a lion *is* in the streets. ¹⁴As the door turneth upon his hinges, so *doth* the slothful upon his bed. ¹⁵The slothful hideth his hand in *his* bosom; it grieveth him to bring it again to his mouth. ¹⁶The sluggard *is* wiser in his own conceit than seven men that can render a reason. ¹⁷He that passeth by, *and* meddleth with strife *belonging* not to him, *is like* one that taketh a dog by the ears. ¹⁸As a mad *man* who casteth firebrands, arrows, and death, ¹⁹So *is* the man *that* deceiveth his neighbour, and saith, Am not I in sport? ²⁰Where no wood is, *there* the fire goeth out: so where *there is* no talebearer, the strife ceaseth. ²¹*As* coals *are* to burning coals, and wood to fire; so *is* a

contentious man to kindle strife. ²²The words of a talebearer *are* as wounds, and they go down into the innermost parts of the belly. ²³Burning lips and a wicked heart *are like* a potsherd covered with silver dross. ²⁴He that hateth dissembleth with his lips, and layeth up deceit within him; ²⁵When he speaketh fair, believe him not: for *there are* seven abominations in his heart. ²⁶*Whose* hatred is covered by deceit, his wickedness shall be shewed before the *whole* congregation. ²⁷Whoso diggeth a pit shall fall therein: and he that rolleth a stone, it will return upon him. ²⁸A lying tongue hateth *those that are* afflicted by it; and a flattering mouth worketh ruin.

27 Boast not thyself of to morrow; for thou knowest not what a day may bring forth. ²Let another man praise thee, and not thine own mouth; a stranger, and not thine own lips. ³A stone *is* heavy, and the sand weighty; but a fool's wrath *is* heavier than them both. ⁴Wrath *is* cruel, and anger *is* outrageous; but who *is* able to stand before envy? ⁵Open rebuke *is* better than secret love. ⁶Faithful *are* the wounds of a friend; but the kisses of an enemy *are* deceitful. ⁷The full soul loatheth an honeycomb; but to the hungry soul every bitter thing is sweet. ⁸As a bird that wandereth from her nest, so *is* a man that wandereth from his place. ⁹Ointment and perfume rejoice the heart: so *doth* the sweetness of a man's friend by hearty counsel. ¹⁰Thine own friend, and thy father's friend, forsake not; neither go into thy brother's house in the day of thy calamity: *for* better *is* a neighbour *that is* near than a brother far off. ¹¹My son, be wise, and make my heart glad, that I may answer him that reproacheth me. ¹²A prudent *man* foreseeth the evil, *and* hideth himself; *but* the simple pass on, *and* are punished. ¹³Take his garment that is surety for a stranger, and take a pledge of him for a strange woman. ¹⁴He that blesseth his friend with a loud voice, rising early in the morning, it shall be counted a curse to him. ¹⁵A continual dropping in a very rainy day and a contentious woman are alike. ¹⁶Whosoever hideth her hideth the wind, and the ointment of his right hand, *which* bewrayeth *itself.* ¹⁷Iron sharpeneth iron; so a man sharpeneth the countenance of his friend. ¹⁸Whoso keepeth the fig tree shall eat the fruit thereof: so he that waiteth on his master shall be honoured. ¹⁹As in water face *answereth* to face, so the heart of man to man. ²⁰Hell and destruction are never full; so the eyes of man are never satisfied. ²¹*As* the fining pot for silver, and the furnace for gold; so *is* a man to his praise. ²²Though thou shouldest bray a fool in a mortar among wheat with a pestle, *yet* will not his foolishness depart from him. ²³Be thou diligent to know the state of thy flocks, *and* look well to thy herds. ²⁴For riches *are* not for ever: and doth the crown *endure* to every generation? ²⁵The hay appeareth, and the tender grass sheweth itself, and herbs of the mountains are gathered. ²⁶The lambs *are* for thy clothing, and the goats *are* the price of the field. ²⁷And *thou shalt have* goats' milk enough for thy food, for the food of thy household, and *for* the maintenance for thy maidens.

28 The wicked flee when no man pursueth: but the righteous are bold as a lion. ²For the transgression of a land many *are* the princes thereof: but by a man of understanding *and* knowledge the state *thereof* shall be prolonged. ³A poor

man that oppresseth the poor *is like* a sweeping rain which leaveth no food. ⁴They that forsake the law praise the wicked: but such as keep the law contend with them. ⁵Evil men understand not judgment: but they that seek the LORD understand all *things*. ⁶Better *is* the poor that walketh in his uprightness, than *he that is* perverse *in his* ways, though he *be* rich. ⁷Whoso keepeth the law *is* a wise son: but he that is a companion of riotous *men* shameth his father. ⁸He that by usury and unjust gain increaseth his substance, he shall gather it for him that will pity the poor. ⁹He that turneth away his ear from hearing the law, even his prayer *shall be* abomination. ¹⁰Whoso causeth the righteous to go astray in an evil way, he shall fall himself into his own pit: but the upright shall have good *things* in possession. ¹¹The rich man *is* wise in his own conceit; but the poor that hath understanding searcheth him out. ¹²When righteous *men* do rejoice, *there is* great glory: but when the wicked rise, a man is hidden. ¹³He that covereth his sins shall not prosper: but whoso confesseth and forsaketh *them* shall have mercy. ¹⁴Happy *is* the man that feareth alway: but he that hardeneth his heart shall fall into mischief. ¹⁵*As* a roaring lion, and a ranging bear; *so is* a wicked ruler over the poor people. ¹⁶The prince that wanteth understanding *is* also a great oppressor: *but* he that hateth covetousness shall prolong *his* days. ¹⁷A man that doeth violence to the blood of *any* person shall flee to the pit; let no man stay him. ¹⁸Whoso walketh uprightly shall be saved: but *he that is* perverse *in his* ways shall fall at once. ¹⁹He that tilleth his land shall have plenty of bread: but he that followeth after vain *persons* shall have poverty enough. ²⁰A faithful man shall abound with blessings: but he that maketh haste to be rich shall not be innocent. ²¹To have respect of persons *is* not good: for for a piece of bread *that* man will transgress. ²²He that hasteth to be rich *hath* an evil eye, and considereth not that poverty shall come upon him. ²³He that rebuketh a man afterwards shall find more favour than he that flattereth with the tongue. ²⁴Whoso robbeth his father or his mother, and saith, *It is* no transgression; the same *is* the companion of a destroyer. ²⁵He that is of a proud heart stirreth up strife: but he that putteth his trust in the LORD shall be made fat. ²⁶He that trusteth in his own heart is a fool: but whoso walketh wisely, he shall be delivered. ²⁷He that giveth unto the poor shall not lack: but he that hideth his eyes shall have many a curse. ²⁸When the wicked rise, men hide themselves: but when they perish, the righteous increase.

29 He, that being often reproved hardeneth *his* neck, shall suddenly be destroyed, and that without remedy. ²When the righteous are in authority, the people rejoice: but when the wicked beareth rule, the people mourn. ³Whoso loveth wisdom rejoiceth his father: but he that keepeth company with harlots spendeth *his* substance. ⁴The king by judgment establisheth the land: but he that receiveth gifts overthroweth it. ⁵A man that flattereth his neighbour spreadeth a net for his feet. ⁶In the transgression of an evil man *there is* a snare: but the righteous doth sing and rejoice. ⁷The righteous considereth the cause of the poor: *but* the wicked regardeth not to know *it*. ⁸Scornful men bring a city into a snare: but wise *men* turn away wrath. ⁹*If* a wise man contendeth with a foolish man, whether he rage or laugh, *there is* no rest. ¹⁰The bloodthirsty hate the upright: but the just seek his soul. ¹¹A fool uttereth all his mind: but a wise *man* keepeth it in till afterwards. ^{12}If a ruler hearken to lies, all his servants *are* wicked. ^{13}The poor and the deceitful man meet together: the LORD lighteneth both their eyes. ^{14}The king that faithfully judgeth the poor, his throne shall be established for ever. ^{15}The rod and reproof give wisdom: but a child left *to himself* bringeth his mother to shame. ^{16}When the wicked are multiplied, transgression increaseth: but the righteous shall see their fall. ^{17}Correct thy son, and he shall give thee rest; yea, he shall give delight unto thy soul. ^{18}Where *there is* no vision, the people perish: but he that keepeth the law, happy *is* he. ^{19}A servant will not be corrected by words: for though he understand he will not answer. ^{20}Seest thou a man *that is* hasty in his words? *there is* more hope of a fool than of him. ^{21}He that delicately bringeth up his servant from a child shall have him become *his* son at the length. ^{22}An angry man stirreth up strife, and a furious man aboundeth in transgression. ^{23}A man's pride shall bring him low: but honour shall uphold the humble in spirit. ^{24}Whoso is partner with a thief hateth his own soul: he heareth cursing, and bewrayeth *it* not. ^{25}The fear of man bringeth a snare: but whoso putteth his trust in the LORD shall be safe. ^{26}Many seek the ruler's favour; but *every* man's judgment *cometh* from the LORD. ^{27}An unjust man *is* an abomination to the just: and *he that is* upright in the way *is* abomination to the wicked.

30

The words of Agur the son of Jakeh, *even* the prophecy: the man spake unto Ithiel, even unto Ithiel and Ucal, ^{2}Surely I *am* more brutish than *any* man, and have not the understanding of a man. ^{3}I neither learned wisdom, nor have the knowledge of the holy. ^{4}Who hath ascended up into heaven, or descended? who hath gathered the wind in his fists? who hath bound the waters in a garment? who hath established all the ends of the earth? what *is* his name, and what *is* his son's name, if thou canst tell? ^{5}Every word of God *is* pure: he *is* a shield unto them that put their trust in him. ^{6}Add thou not unto his words, lest he reprove thee, and thou be found a liar. ^{7}Two *things* have I required of thee; deny me *them* not before I die: ^{8}Remove far from me vanity and lies: give me neither poverty nor riches; feed me with food convenient for me: ^{9}Lest I be full, and deny *thee,* and say, Who *is* the LORD? or lest I be poor, and steal, and take the name of my God *in vain.* ^{10}Accuse not a servant unto his master, lest he curse thee, and thou be found guilty. ^{11}*There is* a generation *that* curseth their father, and doth not bless their mother. ^{12}*There is* a generation *that are* pure in their own eyes, and *yet* is not washed from their filthiness. ^{13}*There is* a generation, O how lofty are their eyes! and their eyelids are lifted up. ^{14}*There is* a generation, whose teeth *are as* swords, and their jaw teeth *as* knives, to devour the poor from off the earth, and the needy from *among* men. ^{15}The horseleach hath two daughters, *crying,* Give, give. There are three *things that are* never satisfied, *yea,* four *things* say not, It is enough: ^{16}The grave; and the barren womb; the earth *that* is not filled with water; and the fire *that* saith not, It is enough. ^{17}The eye *that* mocketh at *his* father, and despiseth to obey *his* mother, the ravens of the valley shall pick it out, and the young eagles shall eat it. ^{18}There be three *things which* are too wonderful for me, yea, four which I know not: ^{19}The way of an eagle in the air; the way of a serpent upon a rock; the way of a ship in the midst of the sea; and the way of a man with a maid. ^{20}Such *is* the way of an adulterous woman; she eateth, and wipeth her mouth, and saith, I have done no wickedness. ²¹For three *things* the earth is disquieted, and for four *which* it cannot bear: ²²For a servant when he reigneth; and a fool when he is filled with meat; ²³For an odious *woman* when she is married; and an handmaid that is heir to her mistress. ²⁴There be four *things which are* little upon the earth, but they *are* exceeding wise: ²⁵The ants *are* a people not strong, yet they prepare their meat in the summer; ²⁶The conies *are but* a feeble folk, yet make they their houses in the rocks; ²⁷The locusts have no king, yet go they forth all of them by bands; ²⁸The spider taketh hold with her hands, and is in kings' palaces. ²⁹There be three *things* which go well, yea, four are comely in going: ³⁰A lion *which is* strongest among beasts, and turneth not away for any; ³¹A greyhound; an he goat also; and a king, against whom *there is* no rising up. ³²If thou hast done foolishly in lifting up thyself, or if thou hast thought evil, *lay* thine hand upon thy mouth. ³³Surely the churning of milk bringeth forth butter, and the wringing of the nose bringeth forth blood: so the forcing of wrath bringeth forth strife.

31

The words of king Lemuel, the prophecy that his mother taught him. ²What, my son? and what, the son of my womb? and what, the son of my vows? ³Give not thy strength unto women, nor thy ways to that which destroyeth kings. ⁴*It is* not for kings, O Lemuel, *it is* not for kings to drink wine; nor for princes strong drink: ⁵Lest they drink, and forget the law, and pervert the judgment of any of the afflicted. ⁶Give strong drink unto him that is ready to perish, and wine unto those that be of heavy hearts. ⁷Let him drink, and forget his poverty, and remember his misery no more. ⁸Open thy mouth for the dumb in the cause of all such as are appointed to destruction. ⁹Open thy mouth, judge righteously, and plead the cause of the poor and needy.

¹⁰Who can find a virtuous woman? for her price *is* far above rubies. ¹¹The heart of her husband doth safely trust in her, so that he shall have no need of spoil. ¹²She will do him good and not evil all the days of her life. ¹³She seeketh wool, and flax, and worketh willingly with her hands. ¹⁴She is like the merchants' ships; she bringeth her food from afar. ¹⁵She riseth also while it is yet night, and giveth meat to her household, and a portion to her maidens. ¹⁶She considereth a field, and buyeth it: with the fruit of her hands she planteth a vineyard. ¹⁷She girdeth her loins with strength, and strengtheneth her arms. ¹⁸She perceiveth that her merchandise *is* good: her candle goeth not out by night. ¹⁹She layeth her hands to the spindle, and her hands hold the distaff. ²⁰She stretcheth out her hand to the poor; yea, she reacheth forth her hands to the needy. ²¹She is not afraid of the snow for her household: for all her household *are* clothed with scarlet. ²²She maketh herself coverings of tapestry; her clothing *is* silk and purple. ²³Her husband is known in the gates, when he sitteth among the elders of the land. ²⁴She maketh fine linen, and selleth *it;* and delivereth girdles unto the merchant. ²⁵Strength and honour *are* her clothing; and she shall rejoice in time to come. ²⁶She openeth her mouth with wisdom; and in her tongue *is* the law of kindness. ²⁷She looketh well to the ways of her household, and eateth not the bread of idleness. ²⁸Her children arise up, and call her blessed; her husband *also,* and he praiseth her. ²⁹Many daughters have done virtuously,

but thou excellest them all. [30]Favour *is* deceitful, and beauty *is* vain: *but* a woman *that* feareth the LORD, she shall be praised. [31]Give her of the fruit of her hands; and let her own works praise her in the gates.

Manufactured by Amazon.ca
Bolton, ON